Miami South Beach

THE Delaplaine 2019
LONG WEEKEND GUIDE

Andrew Delaplaine

NO BUSINESS HAS PAID A SINGLE PENNY OR GIVEN ANYTHING TO BE INCLUDED IN THIS BOOK.

A list of the author's other travel guides, as well as his political thrillers and titles for children, can be found at the end of this book.

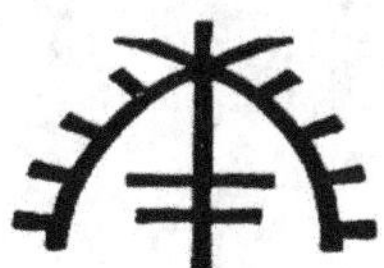

Senior Editors – **Renee & Sophie Delaplaine**
Senior Writer – **James Cubby**
Art Director – **Chip McGoldrick**

Gramercy Park Press
New York – London – Paris

Please submit corrections, additions or comments to andrewdelaplaine@mac.com

Chapter 1
FIRST THINGS FIRST

BY WAY OF INTRODUCTION

Food, Wine & Travel

I've written about food, wine and travel for decades, and while I've lived on South Beach since the late-1980s, most of the writing about food and wine had to do with New York or London or Paris, definitely **not** South Beach. One could write endless "travel" pieces about Miami, but the "food" and "wine" offerings were pretty much limited unless you went to **Joe's Stone Crab** for the food and **The Forge** for the wine.

My, my ... how things have changed.

Miami and South Beach are now year-round destinations. The nightlife industry, the fuel that drives the engine, churns all through the summer, never letting up. Most of the top bars and clubs have licenses that permit them to remain open selling liquor till 5am.

As a butler I once had in London used to say: **Raathuur!**

Chefs from all over the world have established outposts on South Beach, eager to be part of the scene.

Boutique hotels (the **W**, the **Setai**, the **Gale**, etc.) have flooded in and cranked up the quality of service to the 4- and even 5-Star levels. (Trust me, child, it wasn't always like this.)

This really is a world-class town. And in this book I will share some things I like about it (and a few I don't.) This is not a book to tell you how to get from your hometown to Miami International Airport, or from MIA to South Beach. You can figure that out by yourself. (And if you can't, stay home.)

It's also **not a comprehensive book** covering the County. It's not a phone book or something purporting to cover everything. God forbid. Who'd want to read such a book? No. This, like my other **Guides**, is my **personal** take on the scene for visitors, not necessarily residents. Thus, there are no listings for some of the great restaurants I've trekked to in South and West Miami. The listings are intentionally brief, so they can be digested fast.

WHY MIAMI?

Because it may be the most **interesting** city in the U.S. There are probably only a handful of cities in America that offer truly distinctive "feels," and by that I mean

a unique sensation you get when you're there that you don't get anywhere else.

Boston has it, Charleston has it, New York, San Francisco, New Orleans, Chicago, Vegas and a handful of other cities large and small have it. But, to be honest, if you removed my blindfold on a street in Buffalo or Cleveland, I'd have a hard time telling them apart at first glance. (Or even second glance.)

Not so Miami.

And it's not all sex, drugs and rock 'n roll. (Well ... it's not, really.) It's home to some major league cultural institutions, from the **Miami City Ballet** headed by Edward Villella; the **New World Symphony** with topper Michael Tilson Thomas, the stupendously successful **Art Basel**. The off-the-wall collection of tens of thousands of items of decorative and propaganda art assembled by Mickey Wolfson in his **Wolfsonian Museum** now operated by FIU is worth a trip to Miami all by itself. As is the **South Beach Wine & Food Festival** pushed to the top of the heap in its category by the relentless energy of **Lee Brian Schrager.** Schrager and the others have an infectious optimism that has transformed small start-ups into world-class institutions that have made lasting contributions in their fields.

As a young city, these institutions were founded and nurtured by strong-willed individuals. And built from the ground up. If they began with something to prove, they proved it.

But I'm assuming you know why you're coming here. I'm not here to sell you on the town. If it's February, it's probably got a lot more to do with a suntan than with Schumann, and you're probably more interested in a good mojito than Mozart. And you might not care or even know the difference between a Degas and a Duchamp, a Picasso and a Pissarro. And maybe you **are** here because of the sex, drugs and rock 'n roll. Whatever.

Let's face it: how many towns in America let their clubs, bars and dives stay open till 5am selling booze? (And everything else—they don't call it Sodom by the Sea for nuttin'!)

Miami has an edge. And the edge is what's most interesting about it, with the hundred different ethnic influences all mixing together to make it so dramatic, Mozart and the ballet notwithstanding.

TRANSPORTATION & TIPS FOR GETTING AROUND

AIRPORT FLYER

miamidade.gov/transit/routes_detail.asp?route=150

One of the most economical ways to get to the Miami Airport is to take the Airport Flyer, an express bus with service between MIA, Metrorail, and Miami Beach that costs only $2.35. The Airport Flyer runs every half hour from 6 a.m. to 11 p.m. Look for the Airport Flyer signs at bus stops.

SOUTH BEACH TROLLEY

For those visitors traveling around South Beach there is now free trolley service. The South Beach Local bus service has now been replaced by South Beach trolley service. Several loops run daily free of charge: Middle Beach Loop, North Beach Loop, South Beach Loop, and Collins Express. Most trolleys arrive at designated stops every 15 minutes, Collins Express every 20 minutes and South Beach Loop via 10th Street every 35 minutes. Trolleys run 365 days a year, Monday through Saturday 6 a.m. to midnight and 8 a.m. to midnight on Sundays. The citywide service runs from South Pointe Drive to 87 Street. **www.miamibeachfl.gov/city-hall/transportation/trolley/** Download the app on iTunes: **City of Miami Beach e-Gov** then go to **Track the Trolley.**

MIAMI HOP-ON HOP-OFF BUS

hop-on-hop-off-bus.com

Visitors to Miami can travel all over Miami and learn about the city at the same time on one of the many red double-decker Hop-On Hop-Off Buses.

Photo: Citi Bike Miami

Buses travel to Downtown Miami, the Design District, Coconut Grove, Coral Gables and beyond. A two-day pass costs $39 allowing you to hop on and hop off at any stop as many times as you wish. For schedules and list of stops.

BIKES

citibikemiami.com

Since most of South Beach is located within one square mile you'll see locals getting around by skateboard and bicycles. Biking is a viable means of transportation in Miami Beach and there are bicycle stands all over the beach and many well-marked bike lanes. Citibike, a popular bike sharing system that has partnered with the City of Miami Beach, offers approximately 1,000 bikes accessible from 100 stations located throughout Miami Beach. This system allows renters to pick up a bike (a charge card is needed) and the bike can be returned to any of the 100 stations located throughout Miami Beach.

RENTING A CAR? THINK TWICE

We recommend you rent a car only if you're planning on leaving South Beach a lot. Parking is a never-ending hassle, the City writes tickets relentlessly and ruthlessly and just finding parking spots on the weekends is a major pain in the ass.

Since South Beach is so small, we suggest you leave your car parked securely in a city-owned garage and either walk or take short cab rides. Even if you use the valet service when you go to a fancy hotel for a drink, the valet will cost you between $30 and $40.

The valets at restaurants are often **not** a real convenience. When it's busy, it can take quite a bit of time for the valet to retrieve your car. So best advice: cab it everywhere. I live here, and I do.

IF YOUR CAR IS TOWED

And trust me, it **will** be towed if you park in a tow away zone. Towing is a cottage industry in this town. The problem: you won't notice the signs until it's too late. Some businesses watch the often hard-to-see tow away zones very carefully and spy as you park in what will look like an OK place, but is really a tow away zone, and within seconds of you leaving your car, a call is made and you are towed.

The towing companies (there are two of them that have a monopoly) make hundreds of thousands of dollars each year on unsuspecting tourists. The City even gets a kickback (uh, I'm sorry, an "administrative fee") for each car towed. It's a shame, but it's true. In other towns, a tow truck can be thought of as providing a service. Here, it's a predatory act sanctioned by the City to rip you off. So, you've been warned.

When your car is towed, it won't be far away. It will be over on a little street just a few minutes from Lincoln Road on the way to the Venetian Causeway. When you get back to where you left your car, look for the little green sign (that you didn't notice before) posted on a wall and this sign will tell you which company has your car. Call **Tremont Towing, 305-672-2395**, or **Beach Towing, 305-534-2128**, to find out which one has your car and how much it is (it'll be between $100 and $350, depending on the season). Summon **UBER,** and go get your car. Stop by an ATM machine. The buggers only take cash, of course.

Speaking of **UBER**. The absolute best way to enjoy South Beach if you are driving over in your own car or a rental is to park the car in a garage (like the one centrally located just north of Lincoln Road on 17th Street), leave it there and take **UBER.** This is what I do. I leave my car parked in front of my house, especially after 6 or 7 in the evening when it's hard to find a good space and then I take UBER all over town.

UBER

You'll ride in nicer cars for cheaper fares and there's no tipping. If you don't have the Uber ap, download it now on your smartphone and use my code when you sign up and get $20 worth of free rides. Code is – **Andrewd145**

THE BEST CAB COMPANY

Central Cab: 305-532-5555 – is a company based on South Beach, so their drivers always know the best route to take you anywhere. Everywhere you're going is only five or six minutes away on the island. Or use the **UBER** ap (the way I do myself) and save money.

SPECIFIC INFORMATION DURING YOUR VISIT

Check out the listings in the weekly newspaper New Times, which has boxes on every corner, or use your laptop (or increasingly these days, even your cell phone) and go to their web site, **miaminewtimes.com**. The Miami Herald only has a good list in its Friday edition. But they also have comprehensive listings online at **miamiherald.com**.

VISITORS' CENTERS

THE ART DECO WELCOME CENTER

1001 Ocean Drive, Miami Beach, (10th and Ocean), 305-763-8026
mdpl.org/welcome-center/visitors-center/_

Located on Ocean Drive across from the beach, the Art Deco Welcome Center offers visitors a center for information, tours, and a gift shop filled with Miami Beach memorabilia and souvenirs as well as Art Deco gifts and books.

ART DECO TOURS

Learn all about South Beach's historical Art Deco District in a VIP Art Deco Walking Tour. Transport in time back to the 20's, 30's and beyond. Learn about the colorful history and admire unique architecture and design with exclusive access to interiors and rooftops. Elevate the experience with the Art Deco Cocktail tour. For schedule and rates, visit **www.artdecotours.com** or call 305-814-4058.

MIAMI BEACH VISITORS' CENTER (MBVC) AT THE CONVENTION CENTER

530 17TH ST, Miami Beach
305-672-1270. Daily from 10-4.
www.miamibeachguest.com

Enter from the WEST side in the center of the building. Call if you get lost. This state-of-the-art facility offers a multilingual staff along with tourist, business and residential amenities. Their literature rack holds over 200 brochures, magazines, newspapers and maps, calendar of events and visitors' guides full of helpful facts. They offer on-the-spot hotel accommodations, and **20 daily tour excursions.** They are the official distributor of Miami's best attraction pass, the Go Miami Card. They provide the MB chamber of commerce's newest feature, the In Card, which offers tourists and residents money-saving amenities at local businesses. Hotel reservations: **800-666-4519**.

MIAMI BEACH LATIN CHAMBER OF COMMERCE & VISITORS' CENTER

501 Lincoln Road, Miami Beach
305-641-1414
miamibeach.org

Located on the grounds of the 1921 Community Church (worth a stop just to see the church) on Lincoln Road.

MIAMI BEACH GAY & LESBIAN CHAMBER OF COMMERCE

1130 Washington Avenue –
First Floor North / 305-673-4440
gogaymiami.com
In the Old City Hall Building.

Chapter 2
LODGING

SOUTH BEACH

THE HIGH LIFE $$$

Rates usually run $300 or $400++

I'll say right off that my favorite hotel is the Raleigh (currently closed for renovations). Sure, sometimes the upholstery will be flawed, or there is a leaky faucet. But for an Art Deco hotel, you can't beat it. Former Ocean Drive Managing Editor Eric Newill and I have spent many an hour in the little bar off the lobby, and it's still my favorite "small" bar in a town with a lot of big, nasty, noisy ones. They have a new owner, designer Tommy Hilfiger, and we're all scared to death what he might do to "improve" the place.

My second favorite is the **Delano** because... it's just such a scene. Exquisitely conceived and usually run pretty well, too.

I like the **Betsy** on Ocean Drive, just off a complete makeover. And they have owners who really care. They are not trying to fool you. Beautifully done. Dream, tucked away down on an unfortunate sad part of Collins Avenue, is also very good.

If I wanted a newer, more modern place, I'd splurge for the **Setai**. But then I'd probably never leave the place once I checked in, so what's the point?

My other favorite new place is **Vintro**, just behind the Bass Museum. Exquisite, fun, colorful and spacious rooms with a great little restaurant and bar in the lobby and a friendly staff with zero attitude. (You go to Delano to experience the attitude and you go to Vintro to escape it.)

1 HOTEL SOUTH BEACH

1 HOTEL SOUTH BEACH

2341 Collins Ave, Miami Beach
305-604-1000
www.1hotels.com

Newly opened upscale beachfront hotel (formerly the Gansevoort and also the Perry) with 4 outdoor pools including rooftop lounge/pool offering an incredible ocean view. After the $100 million they plowed into this huge resort, one hopes it keeps the same name for more than a year or two. Accommodations are top-notch with sophisticated rooms featuring driftwood on the walls. Amenities include: Complimentary Wi-Fi, 55-inch flat-screen TVs and Nespresso machines. Hotel features high-end restaurant, rooftop bar, fitness center, and direct beach access.

AC HOTEL MIAMI BEACH

2912 Collins Ave, Miami Beach
786-264-4720
www.marriott.com/hotels/travel/miaac-ac-hotel-miami-beach

Located a bit north of South Beach, this hotel, like so many South Beach hotels, offers a great lounge with a happening bar scene. Bar offers a menu of local craft beer, wine on tap, creative cocktails and a bar menu of curated tapas.

DELANO
1685 Collins Ave., Miami Beach
305-672-2000. www.delano-hotel.com
Can't say enough about the place. Love it to stay in. Love it for breakfast. Love it for drinks. Love it for lunch. Love it at night. Right on the beach.

EUROSTARS VINTRO HOTEL
2216 Park Ave (corner of 23rd St), Miami Beach, 305-674-9200
www.eurostarshotels.co.uk
Tucked away over behind the Bass Museum within walking distance of the Convention Center is this little gem of a boutique hotel. It's only 2 blocks west of Collins Avenue and the beach. It has just about everything going for it, from an owner who has spared no expense to create an ultra modern property in a gracious Art Deco property. I especially like the colors they use in the rooms (and the small pool area on the roof where there's always a nice breeze). Lots of yellows, oranges, turquoises—bright tropical Caribbean colors that cheer you up the minute you walk into the room. (The single rooms are around 250 square feet, but they have 1 and 2-bedroom suites as well that are much larger.) The bedding is all 100% Egyptian cotton. Crisp and comfy.

LOEWS
1601 Collins Ave., Miami Beach
305-604-1601
www.loewshotels.com
Standard issue modern hotel. No real character. The 10 or 15 different design elements they threw together in the lobby makes the place look like the inside of a goat's stomach. Somebody was high.

LORD BALFOUR SOUTH BEACH
350 Ocean Dr., Miami Beach
305-673-0401
www.lordbalfourmiami.com
Formerly the Wave Hotel, this 64-room 1940 hotel has been transformed into an art-filled boutique hotel. Attracting the hip and trendy crowd, the hotel amenities include: complimentary Wi-Fi, 40" HD TVs and IPod/iPhone with alarm clock. Located south of historic district but close to clubs/restaurants like Nikki Beach and Prime 112.

METROPOLITAN BY COMO, MIAMI BEACH

2445 Collins Ave., Miami Beach
305-695-3600
www.comohotels.com/metropolitanmiamibeach

This rebuilt Art Deco hotel – the former Traymore Hotel – with a new look and brand (COMO has locations in London, Bangkok, Maldives and Turks & Caicos). The newly opened 74-room hotel is located in the heart of Miami Beach historic district and offers modern luxury. Guests can enjoy complimentary Wi-Fi, swimming pool, 24-hour fitness center and on-site Traymore restaurant.

MONDRIAN

1100 West Ave., Miami Beach
305-514-1500
www.mondrian-miami.com

Now this place has got to be seen – the interior is stunning, but it's still copycat Delano-esque with its use of white. (The same company owns this property.) Unlike any of the other hotels on my list, this one is located on West Avenue overlooking the Bay, so you get a stunning sunset every day.

NAUTILUS

1825 Collins Ave, Miami Beach
305-503-5700
www.sixtyhotels.com

This hotel was originally designed by the famed architect Morris Lapidus (known more for the Fontainebleau and the Eden Roc further up Collins Avenue, whose lobbies, by the way, you really ought to make a special trip to see), this place has been updated and redesigned as an upscale SIXTY hotel (a hip new chain) featuring 250 elegant guestrooms including 51 suites and a two-bedroom Penthouse. A couple of Lapidus features are preserved in the 25-foot high lobby—the sunken bar, very 1950s, and the "stairway to nowhere." Lapidus often installed a flight of stairs in his lobbies, even if when you got to the top of the stairs there was only a wall. Amenities include: balconies, flat-screen TVs, and complimentary Wi-Fi. The hotel is located 650 feet from the beach and features a salt-water pool flanked by cabanas, day-beds and a nice poolside bar; sun terrace; live entertainment; on-site chef-driven dining and a lounge that attracts not only me, but a hip crowd as well. (I'm the one in the corner.)

PRIME HOTEL
100 Ocean Dr., Miami Beach
305-532-0553
www.primehotel-miami.com
This 14-room boutique hotel is located where the trendy restaurant Prime 112 is. Has a stunning rooftop pool, state-of-the-art in-room entertainment, and luxurious furnishings and bathrooms. Very luxe.

RALEIGH (Closed for Renovations)
1775 Collins Ave., Miami Beach
305-534-6300
www.raleighhotel.com/
My favorite hotel on South Beach. I've been haunting its intimate lobby bar ever since Ken Zarrilli bought the property (in 1991, if memory serves) and began the laborious process of restoring it. He sold out for millions to Andre Balazs, and he sold it in 2010 (He still owns the Standard over on the Venetian Causeway.). A Japanese concern bought it, and now it's owned by designer Tommy Hilfiger. We're all scared to death what he's going to do to "improve" the property, but for now, it's still quite special. There's a certain something about this place that when you walk into the lobby, you really feel as if you've been transported back to the 1940s. It's a fleeting sensation, of course, that only lasts for a minute or so, but it's the only place on South Beach where you'll get it at all. Do yourself a favor and walk around the pool—it's the most striking pool in the whole town and deserves to be seen.

THE REDBURY SOUTH BEACH
1776 Collins Ave., Miami Beach
305-604-1776
www.theredbury.com/southbeach
This rebirth of the former Fairfax hotel which sat vacant for years has now been transformed into a hip new 69-room boutique hotel. Named after its hot sister location in Hollywood, Calif, this new venue boasts a rock and roll theme mixed with old school Miami Beach glamor. Checkout the scene around the rooftop pool and taste the delicious handmade pasta, pizza, and other Italian favorites from James Beard Award-winning chef Tony Mantuano in the on-site eatery Lorenzo. Guests are granted access to the Raleigh Hotel's beach and SLS Hotel's fitness facilities.

SAGAMORE

1671 Collins Ave., Miami Beach
305-535-8088
www.sagamorehotel.com

I just love the name "Sagamore." Always have. Back in the late '80s, I used to eat cheap chicken wings and gulp down cold oysters by the dozen at the tacky tiki hut overlooking the ocean by the two swimming pools (one had salt water, one had fresh). The place was full of poor people and deadbeats. Nowadays, the poor people are gone (along with the tiki hut, the salt water pool and the low prices), but it's a gorgeous place.

SETAI

2001 Collins Ave., Miami Beach
305-520-6000 www.thesetaihotel.com

Ultimate in luxury. The only thing I don't like about the Setai is that they've created such an enclosed environment that you don't really feel like you're on South Beach at all. Their lavish Sunday brunch is perhaps the most expensive one in town. But it's HUGE. Don't plan on eating for a day ahead or a day after you slog through this food-fest.

SHORE CLUB

1901 Collins Ave., Miami Beach
305-695-3100
www.shoreclub.com

Was a hot spot till it was eclipsed by the W and the Gale. Owned by the same company that owns the Delano and the Mondrian over on West Avenue, so everything's really quite tip-top. There's a lot of activity here at night, what with the trendy Skybar packing 'em in.

SLS HOTEL SOUTH BEACH

1701 Collins Ave., Miami Beach
305-674-1701
www.slshotels.com/southbeach

Elegant, chic newly refurbished luxury hotel with an incredibly unimaginative name. SLS? Who came up with that? But it's a hotbed of hip activity. A Philippe Starck creation with assistance from names like Lenny Kravitz. Beautiful hotel & two pools with top-notch restaurants. $$$$

THE STANDARD

40 Island Ave., Miami Beach
305-673-1717
www.standardhotel.com

With so many of the first class hotels offering spas, there's no real reason to come off South Beach (this place is located on the first island of the Venetian Causeway, just over a short bridge from South Beach). But it is on the water on Biscayne Bay, and that makes it very nice. Another good thing about it is that it IS off South Beach, and quiet at night, so you don't have any of the noise and nonsense and kids throwing beer bottles at each other when they pour out of the clubs at 3 or 4 a.m. Owned by Andre Balazs, who sold the Raleigh in 2010 but in his grand hotel empire decided to keep this nice and subdued place on South Beach.

W SOUTH BEACH

2201 Collins Ave., Miami Beach
305-938-3000
www.wsouthbeach.com

What can I say that other people haven't said? They spared no expense, and it's clear they want you to notice it. A little pretentious in that sense. Here, don't forget, you have one of the hippest scenes playing out in all its shallowness on South Beach right now: you have Mr. Chow. You have the Club Wall (with only table service, it's a real "experience" watching the chemistry of young girls circle the moneyed bozos at the tables). But the rooms are lovely, the service so-so. It can be flawless one day, and then the very next day, totally crummy.

VICTOR

1144 Ocean Dr., Miami Beach
305-779-8700
www.hotelvictorsouthbeach.com

Of the three hotels I list on Ocean Drive, this is the trendiest, hippest. DJs playing on weekend, lots of parties. A gorgeously restored Art Deco gem. When you're in the lobby, you feel like you're on an ocean liner in the 1930s. Second story pool deck lots of fun.

THE MIDDLE GROUND $$

These properties are in the medium range in terms of price, but still offer something special.

ALBION
1650 James Ave., Miami Beach
305-913-1000
www.rubellhotels.com
Charming property in a lovingly refurbished Art Deco masterpiece (a perfect example of the sub-genre known as "Nautical Deco"). Owned by the famous Rubell Family, important art collectors relocated from New York who were among the vanguard that made Miami an accepted art Mecca. Worth stopping in just to look at the stunning lobby and the above-ground pool with portholes in the side. On the corner of Lincoln road, so it's perfectly located in the heart of South Beach.

THE ANGLER'S RESORT
660 Washington Ave., Miami Beach:
305-534-9600
www.theanglersresort.com
Tucked away on lower Washington Avenue is this upscale little hotel you'd never know about unless someone told you. They've taken a couple Art Deco gems built in the '30s by architect Henry Maloney, completely refurbished them, and then added a couple of spanking new buildings to complement the old Mediterranean Revival style Maloney used on the old buildings. The combination of design elements really works here. Lots of little nooks and crannies make the place very intimate. A very fine restaurant, 600 at The Angler's, is on the premises. Lovely little bar.

AVALON HOTEL
700 Ocean Dr., Miami Beach
800-933-3306
http://www.avalonhotel.com
Classic Art Deco best describes this hotel. The epicenter of Ocean Drive, it features a fabulous ambiance buzzing with energy, newly renovated guest rooms. Home to the award-winning, AAA Four-Diamond A Fish Called Avalon, renowned for serving up the freshest seafood.

THE BETSY
1440 Ocean Dr., Miami Beach
305-531-6100
www.thebetsyhotel.com
If I had to stay on Ocean Drive this year, I'd stay here. 63 rooms. Professional, clean, painstakingly decorated and

THE BETSY

maintained, you'll love the lobby with its elegant yet relaxed tropical Colonial décor. You almost expect Somerset Maugham or Noel Coward to walk through the front door. Great restaurant in lobby, LT Steak & Seafood. Nicely done rooftop for getting sun. They now have a bridge that connects to an art deco hotel on Collins Ave adding rooms and a rooftop pool.

DREAM
1111 Collins Ave., Miami Beach
305-673-4747
www.dreamsouthbeach.com
They took the Tudor Hotel and Palmer House and converted them into this property with 108 rooms and suites. Rooftop pool and lounge. In what is NOT the chicest part of Collins Avenue, this place ranks as the best hotel in the area. They've spared no expense.

GALE SOUTH BEACH & REGENT HOTEL
1690 Collins Ave., Miami Beach
305-673-0199 www.galehotel.com
Two 1940s Art Deco hotels connected and beautifully refurbished. Boutique atmosphere with 87 guest rooms, Regent Cocktail Club and 5,000 square-foot pool deck.

GAYTHERING

GAYTHERING

1409 Lincoln Rd, Miami Beach
786-284-1176
www.gaythering.com

This is Miami Beach's only "straight friendly" hotel. Located in South Beach in the neighborhood where the trendy Lincoln Road meets the Bay. Amenities include: complimentary Wi-Fi, hypoallergenic bedding, 40" HDTV, walk-in showers, and sleep sound machines. The lobby area offers a communal space where guests and locals can "gayther" for coffee, a drink or a bite to eat. Inside the hotel, you'll find a coffee shop, a lounge, a library, and a "Do It Yourself Spa" (which includes Hamam, Jacuzzi, Steam Room and Sauna). Conveniently located near restaurants, nightlife, attractions and shopping.

HILTON BENTLEY

101 Ocean Dr., Miami Beach
305-938-4600
www.hiltonbentleymiami.com

AAA 4-Diamond hotel, not to be confused with the Bentley on Fifth Street 4 blocks down in quiet SoFi. Each suite has been meticulously designed, fully equipped with 42-inch LCD televisions, stainless steel gourmet kitchenettes, and featuring majestic views of the ocean and Miami Beach. Has Spa 101, as well as the great Prime Italian and Bentley Beach Club.

THE HOTEL

801 Collins Ave., Miami Beach
305-531-2222
www.thehotelofsouthbeach.com

This used to be called The Tiffany, and is now called, simply, The Hotel. Totally redesigned (almost reconceived) by Todd Oldham, from the lobby to the expertly refurbished rooms.

HYATT CENTRIC SOUTH BEACH MIAMI

1600 Collins Ave, Miami Beach
305-428-1234
https://southbeachmiami.centric.hyatt.com/en/hotel/

Hyatt brings its contemporary lifestyle brand to this newly built 10-story glass-tower hotel featuring 105 modern guest rooms. Amenities include: complimentary Wi-Fi and flat-screen TVs. rooftop deck, and fitness center. Hotel features include: Spanish-Mediterranean eatery, rooftop deck, and fitness center. Smoke-free hotel.

MARRIOTT STANTON

161 Ocean Dr., Miami Beach
305-536-7700
www.miamibeachmarriott.com

This deluxe oceanfront Art Deco hotel is located on Ocean Drive down in SoFi (South of Fifth), the more civilized part of Ocean Drive. Anywhere north of Fifth Street is a zoo. Balconies with magnificent views. Starbucks and Deco Blue Bar located on-site as well as a great restaurant.

THE PELICAN

826 Ocean Dr., Miami Beach
305-673-3373.
www.pelicanhotel.com

While it took Diesel Jeans owner Renzo Rosso until 1996 to finally open a store on Lexington Avenue in New York, he has been on South Beach much longer, buying this hotel in the early '90s, as I vaguely recall. There's a huge penthouse suite with a Jacuzzi where I've been to many parties. Each room has a kind of wacky theme to it, and this is about the least Art Deco-y hotel on South Beach. But it sure is fun.

ROYAL PALM
1545 Collins Ave, Miami Beach
305-604-5700
www.royalpalmsouthbeach.com
After a $42 million renovation, this has become one of the newest "it" hotels of South Beach. This modern hotel complex offers modern suites, studios and apartments decorated in blends of whites and tropical colors. Amenities include: two swimming pools, beach access, play space for children, complimentary Wi-Fi throughout the hotel, 24-hour Fitness Center, 24-hour concierge, triple distilled and water refreshed daily. On-site full service spa, coffee bar, and two restaurants. Conveniently located near nightlife, restaurants, attractions and shopping. Pets welcomed and non-smoking rooms available.

SANCTUARY
1745 James Ave., Miami Beach
305-673-5455
www.galehotel.com
Two blocks from Lincoln Road, close to the water, very sleek room décor.

SENSE
400 Ocean Dr., Miami Beach
305-538-5529
www.sensebeachhouse.com/
Ultra-modern property on Ocean Drive. Very swank.

SOUTH BEACH MARRIOTT
161 Ocean Dr., Miami Beach
305-536-7700
www.miamibeachmarriott.com
This deluxe oceanfront Art Deco hotel is located on Ocean Drive in South Beach - America's Riviera. Balconies with magnificent views. Starbucks and Deco Blue Bar located on-site.

STILES HOTEL
1120 Collins Ave, Miami Beach
877-538-9299

www.thestileshotel.com
Art deco inspired hotel with 54 retro-chic rooms and suites located in the center of the Art Deco district. Amenities include: flat-screen TVs, complimentary Wi-Fi, iPod docks, rainfall showers, and DVD players. Two onsite restaurants and garden with 3 swimming pools. Free parking.

SURFCOMBER
1717 Collins Ave., Miami Beach
305-532-7715. www.surfcomber.com
If you want to be near the Delano or the Raleigh, but don't want to pay the arm and a leg required to be inside those two posh properties, this is your best bet. It's right on the beach—just like its ritzier neighbors—and has all the amenities. Everything's a short walk from this centrally located property.

TOWNHOUSE
150 20th St., Miami Beach
305-534-3800
www.townhousehotel.com
Great rooftop bar. On the oceanfront. Conceived as a cool place to chill out, this hotel opened its doors in 2000 with a playful combination of modern design and homey comfort. Built in 1939, the five-story building has been creatively redefined by Paris-based designer India Mahdavi. Her flirty, quirky design achieves an edgy and fun atmosphere without sacrificing comfort for style's sake. The brand new renovated Rooftop Lounge is great for events or photo shoots.

Z OCEAN
1437 Collins Ave., Miami Beach
305-672-4554
www.zoceanhotelsouthbeach.com
Nestled on the north end of world-famous Ocean Drive, this hotel offers a chic and intimate haven, as well as access to vibrant, see-and-be-seen nightlife. The suites feature luxurious California King size beds complemented by a memorable walk-in shower experience. Oversized private terraces provide the perfect setting to enjoy the hustle and bustle of South Beach. The hotel is an intimate affair, offering impeccable service, quality and location right on Miami Beach.

CHEAPER ALTERNATIVES $

Rates usually run below $200

The problem with South Beach is there's not much of a "middle ground" when it comes to lodgings. You either have these high-priced luxury hotels or row after row of much lower-end choices. There are dozens of hotels lining Collins Avenue below 20th Street, but they're mostly hit or miss. The rooms are small, the walls are thin, the windows are old and not soundproofed and don't protect you from the endless noise coming from Collins Avenue, partiers are coming in at all hours... well, you get the picture. There are faults with most of these hotels, so I will point out the benefits, besides price.

BENTLEY HOTEL
510 Ocean Dr., Miami Beach
305-538-1700
www.thebentleyhotel.com
Nice enough property, but it's on the busiest corner you can imagine where every car coming off the Causeway turns onto Ocean Drive.

CATALINA
1732-1756 Collins Ave., Miami Beach
305-674-1160
www.catalinahotel.com
The owners have cobbled together three buildings on bustling Collins Avenue to form the Catalina. Cheap rooms, but nicely maintained. Always busy. Has a happening restaurant and bar scene as well.

CHELSEA
944 Washington Ave., Miami Beach
305-534-4069
www.thehotelchelsea.com
Has a nice restaurant and cozy bar, across from the Wolfsonian Museum. Rooms are spotless the two times I was in them, staff friendly.

CLEVELANDER HOTEL

CHESTERFIELD HOTEL & SUITES

855 Collins Ave., Miami Beach
305-531-5831
www.thechesterfieldhotel.com

Art Deco-design hotel has been completely renovated to modern standards. Animal prints abound in a funky South Beach style that fills the hotel. Complimentary transfers to and from the airport.

CLEVELANDER HOTEL

1020 Ocean Dr., Miami Beach
305-532-4006
www.clevelander.com

Has 60 revamped rooms and ROCKSTAR Suites, two rooftop decks with ocean-front and city views, enhanced poolside bars, and a new café-style menu. The 1937 art deco landmark famous for its fun parties, year-round is back stronger than ever showcasing the hottest DJ's, bands, dancers, musicians, models and performance groups. Gets rowdy on weekends.

ESSEX HOUSE

1001 Collins Ave., Miami Beach
305-534-2700
www.essexhotel.com

This property is in a very busy part of Collins Avenue that's a bit much for me. But this property is a good bargain. Also, even if you don't stay here, slip into the lobby for a look at its Art Deco lobby that has some unusual Egyptian motifs that will have you scratching your head.

OCEAN FIVE HOTEL

436 Ocean Dr., Miami Beach
305-532-7093
www.oceanfive.com

This unpretentious boutique hotel is down in the tranquil SoFi (South of Fifth).

RICHMOND HOTEL

1757 Collins Ave., Miami Beach
305-538-2331
www.richmondhotel.com

Designed in the early 1940s by L. Murray Dixon, this oceanfront Art Deco masterpiece offers luxurious accommodations with state-of-the-art amenities. Relax on the stunning pool deck or in the coconut palm tropical garden, or take a few steps onto the white sandy beach. Experience the charm and energy of South Beach while staying at this private, secluded and elegant hotel.

RIVIERA

318 20th St., Miami Beach
305 538-7444
www.rivierahotelsouthbeach.com/

A few blocks from Lincoln Road and a couple of blocks from the ocean. This Miami Beach 1940's classic was transformed into a boutique hideaway for jetsetters and trendsetters alike. Inspired by the modern baroque designs of Dorothy Draper, the hotel combines Hollywood Regency touches with the hotel group's signature bold and modern designs.

SEAGULL HOTEL MIAMI BEACH
100 21st St., Miami Beach
305-538-6631
www.seagullhotelmiamibeach.com/
Directly on the beach with sweeping views of the Atlantic. It is a cozy, tropical hotel with exotic murals and oversized rattan furniture. All nonsmoking guest rooms with free Wi-Fi. Within walking distance of Lincoln Road.

SOUTH SEAS HOTEL
1751 Collins Ave., Miami Beach
305-538-1411
www.southseashotel.com
Excellent location right in the middle of the action. Nothing fancy.

WINTER HAVEN
1400 Ocean Dr., Miami Beach
305-531-5571
www.winterhavenhotelsobe.com
71 welcoming guest rooms. Hotel offers a variety of ocean views, an Ocean Drive patio and Martini bar, daily breakfast, Wi-Fi throughout, beach towels and chairs, multilingual staff, rooftop sundeck, and use of the pool at the sister Blue Moon Hotel.

MIDDLE BEACH / NORTH BEACH

All these hotels share one thing in common: they're NOT on South Beach. So if it's a more tranquil environment you're looking for, this is the place to stay. You're only 5 or 10 minutes (depending on traffic) from South Beach by cab.

CIRCA39 HOTEL
3900 Collins Ave., Miami Beach
305-538-4900
www.circa39.com
Recently renovated. Has a nice eatery on site, Jules Kitchen.

CASA FAENA
3500 Collins Ave., Miami Beach
786-646-1250
www.faena.com/Casa-Faena/
Originally built in 1928, this has been recently restored. Has volcanic rock columns, Spanish Colonial art, and an in-lobby splash spa. Rooms and suites overlook an interior courtyard. Italian restaurant on site.

CONFIDANTE
4041 Collins Ave, Miami Beach
305-424-1234
http://theconfidante.unbound.hyatt.com/en/hotel/home.html
One of Miami's newest hotels to open after an $80 million renovation, this unique hotel constructed from three towers of different eras – one a 1940s Art Deco skyscraper—features 380 beautifully decorated rooms. It's one of those places up in Mid Beach that puts it out of everything happening on South Beach, so be sure you know where this place is located before booking. (Me? I'd stay on South Beach and take Uber up here to hang out in the lobby.) Amenities include: complimentary Wi-Fi, flat-screen TVs and minibars. Hotel features include a library-like cocktail lounge, two heated pools, an open-air spa, and a fitness center.

COURTYARD CADILLAC MIAMI BEACH
3925 Collins Ave., Miami Beach
305 538-3373
www.hotelcadillacmiamibeach.com
Experience this hotel's exciting guestroom makeover featuring contemporary design with vibrant colors, sophisticated artistic details and warm woods. Sitting on two oceanfront acres, the hotel allows for breathtaking sunrise or moon-lit walks on the beach. Located less than two miles from South Beach's Art Deco District, the hotel offers both business-travel conveniences and boutique-style elegance with the comfort of resort amenities. Originally known as the Cadillac Hotel, the historic property reopened following a $40 million renovation to include spa services, private tiki beach, balconies on oceanfront guestrooms and much more.

CROYDON
3720 Collins Ave, Miami Beach
305-938-1145

FAENA

www.hotelcroydonmiamibeach.com
Designed in 1937 and formerly known as the Croydon Arms, this fully-renovated seven-story boutique hotel offers 104 guest rooms including a penthouse suite. Amenities include: flat-screen TVs, iPod docks, and complimentary Wi-Fi (in the lobby). Hotel features include: rooftop sundeck, outdoor pool, fitness center & spa. Nightclub & bowling alley on premises. Free airport shuttle and beach chairs.

EDEN ROC
4525 Collins Ave., Miami Beach
305-531-0000
www.edenrocmiami.com
Just off a massive renovation. Iconic lobby bar must be seen. If you have to stay in Middle Beach, this is the place (or next door at the Fontainebleau).

FAENA
3201 Collins Ave, Miami Beach
305-534-8800
www.faena.com/miami-beach
NEIGHBORHOOD: Mid-beach
Hot shot Argentine developer Alan Faena is responsible for this glamorous newly remodeled 1947 resort hotel (It's the old Saxony Hotel) that boasts beautifully designed art deco inspired rooms (58 rooms, 111 suites). He hired moviemaker Baz Luhrmann and his wife Catherine Martin and let them go all-out on this place, which has to be seen to be believed. Luhrmann, you might remember, remade "The Great Gatsby" with DiCaprio. And this hotel is as tarted up as Baz made

FONTAINEBLEAU

Gatsby's Long Island mansion. The venue features a luxury spa, several high-end restaurants, including Pao by Paul Qui (a mix of Asian, Spanish and French influences) and Los Fuegos by Francis Mallmann, an Argentine grill master who cooks over open fires. (Get the rib eye with chimichurri—it'll be the best you've ever had). There's a big pool and a 150-seat cabaret-style theater. The lobby boasts 8 Juan Gatti murals. Outside in the garden is Damien Hirst's "Gone But Not Forgotten," a 24-karat gold & gilded skeleton of a giant woolly mammoth. Amenities include: complimentary Wi-Fi and on-site Fitness Center. Smoke-free hotel. This hotel is part of a six-block empire Faena has built up here in Middle Beach, and like I said, it's worth a short Uber / Lyft ride up here to have a good look at it all.

FONTAINEBLEAU
4441 Collins Ave., Miami Beach
305 538-2000
www.fontainebleau.com/
One of two gloriously kitchy hotels (the other being next door, the Eden Roc) designed by Morris Lapidus. This was back in the mid '50s when Middle Beach became the rising star and South Beach sank into the gutter of neglect. After all, they didn't even have pools at the South Beach hotels. Lapidus more than made up for it.

FREEHAND

(Formerly Indian Creek Hotel)

2727 Indian Creek Dr., Miami Beach
305-531-2727
http://thefreehand.com/

Constructed in 1936, Indian Creek Hotel is my personal favorite up in Middle Beach. It's as close to South Beach as you can get without actually being there. Art Deco masterpiece. Heated pool; 69 rooms. Now a happening upmarket hostel.

LORRAINE HOTEL

2601 Collins Ave., Miami Beach
305-538-7721
www.lorrainehotel.com

For the budget-minded traveler, here are airy and spacious rooms.

MIAMI BEACH EDITION

2901 Collins Ave, Miami Beach
786-257-4500
www.editionhotels.com/miami-beach

Hotelier Ian Schrager and Marriott International have launched this luxury lifestyle hotel in the old Seville Hotel, renovated now into 294 guestrooms, including 28 bungalows and rooftop penthouses. Very posh, of course, like anything Schrager touches. Expect a lively bar scene and lots of activity in the Matador Room, Chef John-Georges Vongerichten's high-end on site eatery. Amenities include: complimentary Wi-Fi, iPod docks, and minibars. Hotel features include: Latin restaurant, outdoor lounge, nightclub, bowling alley, ice rink, spa, and a gym.

MIMOSA HOTEL

6525 Collins Ave., Miami Beach
305-867-5000
www.themimosa.com

Oceanfront boutique hotel.

OCEAN SPRAY
4130 Collins Ave., Miami Beach
305-535-5300
www.oceanspraymiami.com
Totally renovated — retaining its classic 1934 Art Deco exterior and lobby design — with chic, European guest and meeting room furnishings.

SOHO BEACH HOTEL
4385 Collins Ave., Miami Beach
786-507-7900
www.sohobeachhouse.com
Swankest place up in this neighborhood. This private members club, hotel and spa are located on the site of the Sovereign Hotel. The site has been entirely redesigned and expanded to include a 16-story oceanfront tower. Overlooking the ocean, it includes 50 bedrooms, a private beach, and an expansive Cowshed spa and gym. There are two pools, indoor and outdoor dining, secluded gardens, a screening room and Cecconi's restaurant open to the public.

WESTGATE
3611 Collins Ave., Miami Beach
305-532-8831
www.wgsouthbeach.com
This newly renovated beachfront resort is the perfect marriage of quaint intimacy and contemporary comfort.

DOWNTOWN/ BRICKELL

A lot of fancy hotels have populated Miami's Downtown/Brickell Corridor in recent years, helping by their presence to elevate what for decades has been one of the more wretched downtown areas of any major U.S. city. And most of Downtown is still pretty much of an eyesore. But while Downtown still has its undeniably seedy side, none of this is apparent in its selection of hotels.

CONRAD MIAMI
1395 Brickell Ave., Miami
305 503-6500
http://conradhotels3.hilton.com/en/hotels/florida/conrad-miami-MIACICI/index.html
Great location on the Bay, this is Hilton's "upscale" brand. Beautiful surroundings for people doing business with a flare (well, on an expense account). Has a notable spa. The 25th floor is home to Atrio, one of the better restaurants Downtown.

CONRAD MIAMI

COURTYARD BY MARRIOTT

200 SE 2nd Ave., Miami
305 374-3000
www.marriott.com/hotels/travel/miadt-courtyard-miami-downtown-brickell-area

Has 231 rooms with balconies (27 of which are one-bedroom suites). Near Bayside Marketplace, Brickell Avenue Financial District and the Port of Miami. Free high-speed Internet access in guest rooms, and free wireless access in public areas. The hotel works with several companies to provide transportation to the Port of Miami for a fee of $5 per person.

DOUBLETREE BY HILTON GRAND

1717 N. Bayshore Drive, Miami
305 372-0313
www.doubletree3.hilton.com/en/hotels/florida/doubletree-by-hilton-grand-hotel-biscayne-bay-MIABSDT/index.html

Hotel and condo complex up in what is still called Omni Area, 10 blocks north of Downtown. Great views of Biscayne Bay. Offers a full range of amenities. Close to the Port of Miami, shopping, the Downtown Miami Business District.

EPIC HOTEL

270 Biscayne Blvd. Way, Miami
305 424-5226
www.epichotel.com

This top spot is on the Miami River where it meets the Bay. Part of Kimpton Hotels, this boutique hotel epitomizes urban design while offering guests an unmatched level of style and service. This hotel operates on a grand scale with an authenticity that attracts travelers from around the globe.

EUROSTARS LANGFORD

121 SE 1st St, Miami
305-250-0782
www.eurostarshotels.com
NEIGHBORHOOD: Downtown

Formerly the Miami National Bank, this iconic building has been reimagined as a 126-room luxury hotel. This architectural gem has been lovingly preserved and offers high-tech amenities. Rooms come equipped with 48" HD flat-screen TVs, complimentary Wi-Fi, and MP3/iPod docking stations. Hotel features include: on-site restaurant, rooftop bar and lounge, and exercise studio.

FOUR SEASONS

1435 Brickell Ave., Miami
305 358-3535
www.fourseasons.com/miami

Sleek tower of luxurious guest rooms and suites offers sweeping vistas and resort-style amenities.

HOLIDAY INN PORT OF MIAMI

340 Biscayne Blvd., Miami
305 371-4400
https://www.ihg.com

Directly across the street from Bayside Marketplace and opposite the Port of Miami. It is within easy walking distance to the Miami Convention Center, American Airlines Arena, the financial district and Government Center. A MetroMover stop is located behind the parking lot. (This is more important than you think.)

HOTEL BEAUX ARTS MIAMI
255 Biscayne Blvd. Way, 39th Floor, Miami - 305 421-8700
www.hotelbeauxartsmiami.com
This boutique property is so exclusive, most people have never heard of it. About as good as it gets in Downtown. Situated on the 39th floor, this hotel is an architectural masterpiece offering the most discriminating and sophisticated business and leisure traveler dramatic city and bay views with total exclusivity. Entirely outfitted with Bang & Olufsen in-room entertainment systems, the hotel is a private urban retreat providing guests with services such as private check-in and personal escort to one of the 44 ultra-contemporary and lavishly appointed guest rooms and suites.

HOTEL URBANO AT BRICKELL
2500 Brickell Ave., Miami
305-856-5055
www.hotelurbanomiami.com
This hotel offers the ultimate boutique accommodations at moderate prices for both business and leisure. Featuring three floors with 65 stylish guest rooms, which have walk-in showers, balconies or lanais, lovely interiors and free high-speed Internet.

HILTON MIAMI
1601 Biscayne Blvd., Miami
305 374-0000
www.hiltonmiamidowntown.com
A Metromover connection provides convenient access around the city. Shuttle service to the Port of Miami through a company located in the hotel lobby, for a fee with advance reservations. Just minutes from Bayside Marketplace, the Design District and Midtown Miami.

HYATT REGENCY MIAMI
400 SE 2nd Ave., Miami
305 358-1234
https://miami.regency.hyatt.com/en/hotel/home.html
On the scenic Riverwalk attached to the Miami Convention Center. Recently completed a $20 million renovation. Featuring the new Hyatt StayFit TM Fitness Center and newly updated heated outdoor pool. Direct access to MetroMover

for transportation around Downtown and to shopping and area attractions. Conveniently located to the Port of Miami, Bayside Marketplace and American Airlines Arena.

INTERCONTINENTAL MIAMI
100 Chopin Plaza, Miami
305 577-1000
www.icmiamihotel.com
Located on Biscayne Bay, adjacent to Bayside Marketplace and Bayfront Park. Elegantly appointed hotel offers luxurious guest rooms and a full range of first-class facilities.

JW MARRIOTT MARQUIS
255 Biscayne Blvd. Way, Miami
305 421-8600
www.jwmarriottmarquismiami.com
The high-end in the Marriott brand, this is centrally located Downtown, and is notable because Daniel Boulud has his restaurant here.

JW MARRIOTT HOTEL MIAMI
1109 Brickell Ave., Miami
305 329-3500
www.marriott.com/miajw
The "other" Marriott Downtown. It blends the features of a premier conference and meeting facility with excellent service. Elegantly furnished guest rooms and suites offer the finest details, including marble tubs, high-speed Internet and flat-screen televisions. Delicious dining options range from the wine-inspired contemporary cuisine of Isabela's, to the casual fare at La Terraza Cafe and Bar. Relaxation is as close as the luxurious spa and the unique stainless pool.

MANDARIN ORIENTAL
500 Brickell Key Drive, Miami
305 913-8288
www.mandarinoriental.com
A waterfront urban resort located on prestigious Brickell Key, featuring spacious guest rooms and suites, state-of-the-art conference and banquet facilities, a five-star holistic Spa and fitness center, and a world-class on-site Beach Club. The hotel is also affiliated with Brickell Tennis Club and Crandon Golf Course. Lots of celebs stay here, or more often dine here.

MANDARIN ORIENTAL

ME MIAMI

1100 Biscayne Blvd, Miami
786-577-9700
www.melia.com

NEIGHBORHOOD: Downtown

Located in Downtown Miami, this 129 room hotel offers both comfort and convenience to travelers. Amenities include: complimentary Wi-Fi, iPod docks, balconies, and cable TV. Hotel facilities include: 2 outdoor pools, full-service spa, fitness center, poolside bar, and on-site restaurant. Smoke-free and pet-friendly hotel. Conveniently located near attractions like Adrienne Arsht Center for the Performing Arts, Jungle Island, and Perez Art Museum.

RIVER PARK HOTEL & SUITES

100 SE 4th St., Miami, 305-374-5100
www.riverparkhotelandsuites.com

Ideally situated in the heart of Downtown Miami on the Miami River, this upscale property offers suites and hotel rooms, with a full-service restaurant, lounge, business center, wireless Internet in all rooms, gym, pool and valet parking.

W MIAMI

W MIAMI
485 Brickell Ave., Miami
305 503-4400
www.wmiamihotel.com
This boutique hotel is always in the news because so many famous people stay here. Designed by Kelly Wearstler, it juxtaposes elite residential necessities with scene-making dining, roof-raising lounging. Set within the 10-acre Icon Brickell enclave, this urban resort is replete with skyscraping residential towers, two parks, a 28,000-square-foot spa and fitness center, and a two-acre outdoor living room bedecked by a 300-foot long pool, oversized outdoor fireplace, and more lifestyle flights of fancy.

COCONUT GROVE

The Grove was THE place to be before South Beach came roaring along in the mid to late '80s to dominate nightlife and entertainment. The club at the Mutiny (what was the owner's name, Barton Goldberg, right?) was the center of activity, and all nightlife in Miami emanated from the Grove.

After the Mariel Boatlift in '80 deposited thousands of poor Cubans (and a lot of criminals as Castro bragged about emptying his jails on a doofus President Carter), the Grove became even hotter because all the Cuban refugees lived in South Beach, then the poorest part of town (and a good time to buy for those smart enough to see ahead).

Anyway, today the Grove has a lot of empty storefronts for rent, the restaurants

are so-so and the nightlife: nothing to speak of.

Still, many see and appreciate the Grove's unique charm. Its residential areas are among the nicest in town. And the Grove will always have its champions. (Having been born there, I am one of them.)

Its hotels, in the meantime, continue to boast some big names and quality environments for the discriminating traveler.

In fact, the Grove is a great place to go if you want out of frenetic South Beach. And they'd be wise to begin an advertising campaign along the lines of the "Come to Miami and experience the UN-South Beach."

COURTYARD BY MARRIOTT

2649 S. Bayshore Drive, Miami

305 858-2500

www.courtyardmiamicoconutgrove.com

20-floor high-rise building features breathtaking views of Miami and Biscayne Bay. It includes 196 spacious guest rooms, including 20 suites. Complimentary Wi-Fi throughout the hotel. Most guest rooms have balconies.

MAYFAIR HOTEL & SPA

3000 Florida Ave., Coconut Grove

305 441-0000

www.mayfairhotelandspa.com

This landmark hotel has a new Cabana Rooftop Pool & Lounge with cabanas, an infinity chic pool and spectacular views of Biscayne Bay and Miami's skyline.

MUTINY HOTEL

2951 S. Bayshore Drive, Coconut Grove

305 441-2100

http://www.mutinyhotel.com

The scene of many wild nights in the '70s and '80s before South Beach came along to steal away the Grove's thunder. The most decadent place in the Cocaine Cowboy Days. The restaurant (private club) was quite unique, had 3 levels and a famous metal membership card with a pirate face on it. (Don't get me started on those "themed" rooms where everybody partied.)

This place fell into disrepair and has been completely refurbished into a modern property.

Its one- and two-bedroom apartment suites are decorated in a "British Colonial" style featuring rich hardwood furnishings, fine Bay views. Every modern convenience and amenity is available, with separate living/dining areas, including a Queen sleeper sofa in the living room, a fully equipped kitchen and European-style bathrooms; flat screen televisions and more. Many suites offer private balconies with city and water views; many units also offer washer/dryer, complimentary upon request. In-room amenities include: Hair dryer, lighted make-up mirror, Fully Equipped Kitchen, flat screen TVs, iPod clock Radios.

RESIDENCE INN BY MARRIOTT
2835 Tigertail Ave., Coconut Grove
305 285-9303
http://www.residenceinn.com/miaco
An all-suite hotel within walking distance from CocoWalk and the shops, dining and nightlife of the Grove. Free daily buffet breakfast, high-speed Internet access, and evening socials on select days.

RITZ-CARLTON
3300 SW 27th Ave., Coconut Grove
305 644-4680
www.ritzcarlton.com
Yes, there's even a Ritz-Carlton in the Grove to go with the ones in Key Biscayne and South Beach. This one has a charming, villa-like ambience, soaring ceilings, Venetian stucco columns, fragrant roses, a grand fireplace (you won't need THAT in summer!) and picturesque views. Italian cuisine in Bizcaya lounge, renowned for its Mediterranean-influenced fare and contemporary Latin live music every Friday and Saturday, or be pampered in the "boutique Spa."

SONESTA BAYFRONT
2889 Mcfarlane Rd., Coconut Grove
305-529-2828
http://www.sonesta.com/
coconutgrove
Nice place with all the usual amenities. The restaurant on the 8th floor, Panorama offers a wide variety of traditional American and Nuevo-Andean Peruvian cuisine.

RITZ-CARLTON KEY BISCAYNE

KEY BISCAYNE

RITZ-CARLTON
455 Grand Bay Dr., Key Biscayne
305-365-4500
www.ritzcarlton.com
Oceanfront resort with a superior "tropical" ambience. About as far from the South Beach "thing" as you can possibly get without going to Maine. Best thing about this place is the huge (over 20,000 square feet) spa. Excellent tennis facilities and, well—they have just about anything you can imagine (except excitement, unless you're sleeping with one of the staff). Great place to come to recuperate from a facelift.

THE BILTMORE

CORAL GABLES

THE BILTMORE
1200 Anastasia Ave, Coral Gables
855 311-6903
http://www.biltmorehotel.com
This National Historic Landmark is located in the exclusive Coral Gables area. The 273-room hotel reflects classic Italian, Moorish, and Spanish architectural influences spread over 150 acres of tropical landscaping. A favorite of world leaders and notables since its opening in 1926, the hotel offers a restored Donald Ross 18-hole, 71 par championship golf course, tennis, one of the largest hotel pools in the country, private cabanas, a European spa, and an award-winning fitness center. The hotel's dining destinations include the acclaimed Palme d'Or, which Zagat calls one of the best restaurants in the country; and Fontana, an Italian restaurant surrounding the Biltmore fountain.

COURTYARD BY MARRIOTT
2051 Le Jeune Road, Coral Gables
305 443-2301
http://www.courtyard.com/miagb
This hotel is located three blocks from the Coral Gables business district and two miles south of MIA, within walking distance of great shopping, dining and area attractions. It features renovated guest rooms and complimentary airport transportation.

HOTEL ST. MICHEL
162 Alcazar Ave., Coral Gables
305-444-1666
www.hotelstmichel.com
This is a tiny gem (only 28 rooms) right in the heart of things. Feels totally unlike anything in Miami, and is where I prefer to stay when I am forced to be in the Gables. Feels like a country inn. It's in a building that went up in 1926 as the Sevilla Hotel. They have a tour desk, free WiFi, flat-screen TVs, free continental breakfast.

HYATT REGENCY
50 Alhambra Plaza, Coral Gables
305 441-1234
https://coralgables.regency.hyatt.com
An elegant Mediterranean-style hotel inspired by Spain's Alhambra Palace. Newly renovated guest rooms are appointed with luxurious furnishings and offer spacious living areas. Located in the center of Coral Gables and close to dining, shopping and entertainment. Wireless high-speed Internet access is available.

HOTEL COLONNADE
180 Aragon Ave., Coral Gables
305 441-2600
www.hotelcolonnade.com/
Centrally located in the business and retail district of Coral Gables. Recognized by Conde Nast Traveler as one of the top 500 hotels in the world. The hotel has ample meeting space to accommodate groups from 10 to 700 people. The Regus Business Center allows business travelers the opportunity to rent a furnished office in the hotel, with convenient features such as high-speed Internet access.

Chapter 3
RESTAURANTS

INTRODUCTION

The greatest pleasure for me has been to witness first hand the explosion of culinary diversity that has made Greater Miami one of the most interesting "food towns" in the U.S.

Not to take anything away from New Orleans or Charleston or Savannah or any other locale in America that boasts a distinctive cuisine, but I can safely say Miami's offerings are terribly more interesting and culturally engaging than any town in the U.S. besides New York.

Why?

Because the cuisines in New Orleans and places like Baltimore—while among the best America has to offer—are generally quite static. Sorry, folks, but in the end, shrimp and grits are still shrimp and grits. That soft-shelled crab at that little shack on the Chesapeake—it's the same year in and year out.

But when was the last time you went to a restaurant and had Guatemalan food? Or Peruvian.

All right—I admit the cuisines you can expect to find in Miami will have a Latin slant—but what's wrong with that? You'll find such a huge variety of cuisines you've never tried before. You'll travel a long, long way from the black beans and rice of a Cuban meal to a ceviche made by a Peruvian.

The excitement generated by the nightlife industry, climate and cultural diversity one gets in Miami has attracted a Who's Who of famous international chefs. The unqualified success of the Food Network South Beach Wine & Food Festival (directly attributable to the obsessive single-mindedness of Lee Brian Schrager of Southern Wine & Spirits) brought chefs from all over the world to South Beach. Many who came, saw what they liked, and opened outposts in their global empires here on the sandy shores of the Billion Dollar Sandbar.

But a big name in France or New York is no guarantee of success. David Bouley's aptly named "Evolution" in the Ritz-Carlton might have easily been named "Natural Selection" because it closed within a year. South Beach is as tough a town as New York or anywhere else where the public is fickle and the rents are as sky high as a chef's ambition.

But the good news is that there seems to be a new opening every week.

MIAMI-DADE FOOD TOURS

If you don't want to do your homework, consider following a guide as you tour the area. I've done a couple of these and they're really quite fun.

MIAMI CULINARY TOURS

LOCATIONS: Little Havana, South Beach, Miami City Tours: **786-942-8856**
www.miamiculinarytours.com
COST: Rates vary by season (special rates for children, military)

FOOD TOURS OF MIAMI

LOCATIONS: Coral Gables and South Beach
www.foodtoursofmiami.com and **www.pubcrawlofmiami.com**
COST: Rates vary by season (special rates for children, military)

SOUTH BEACH
RIDICULOUSLY EXTRAVAGANT

BAOLI

1908 Collins Ave., Miami Beach
305-674-8822
www.baoli-group.com
CUISINE: French, Italian
DRINKS: Full Bar
SERVING: Dinner
PRICE RANGE: $$$$

As good as the food is, the best thing about Baoli is the charming patio-courtyard with a canopy of shade trees sprinkled with lights that give the place an other-worldly feel. A big menu covers all the bases, from a raw bar to sushi to a great selection of pastas (black truffle risotto) to grilled items (an 18oz grilled rib eye), to seafood (get the bouillabaisse). Oh, that "other-worldly" feel? You'll come back to this world when they bring you the check.

THE BAZAAR BY JOSÉ ANDRÉS SLS HOTEL

BARTON G: THE RESTAURANT
1427 West Ave., Miami Beach
305-672-8881
www.bartongtherestaurant.com
CUISINE: American, Contemporary
DRINKS: Full bar
SERVING: Dinner nightly from 6
The expensive (and expensively famous) creation of Barton G. An experience you won't forget. When you come here, throw caution to the wind and surrender yourself. Worth every penny. (I went there on my birthday and ordered a three-pound lobster tail: we were eating lobster salad for two days!)

THE BAZAAR BY JOSÉ ANDRÉS
SLS HOTEL
1701 Collins Ave., Miami Beach
305-455-2999
www.sbe.com/thebazaar
CUISINE: Tapas/Small Plates, Spanish
DRINKS: Full Bar
SERVING: Dinner
PRICE RANGE: $$$$
The swanky SLS Hotel had to have a big name to headline its "important" restaurant, and it's hardtop top José Andrés. Fun place with a creative menu serving items like Dragonfruit Ceviche and Caprese Salad. Delicious cocktails. Great selection of Serrano and Ibérico hams, Catalan pork sausage, codfish fritters (a specialty), seared scallops. Though I never liked it, everybody raves about the Dulce de Leche dessert.

CASA TUA

CASA TUA

1700 James Ave.; Miami Beach
305-673-1010
www.casatualifestyle.com/miami/
CUISINE: Italian, with a flair
DRINKS: Full bar
SERVING: Lunch weekdays 12pm – 3pm; dinner nightly from 7

Very hot spot. The best food. Upstairs they have a VERY nice lounge, but it's private now. (I used to love the upstairs lounge for a drink or two before dining below.) But plebeians can still get in for lunch and dinner. But the food doesn't get much better. A lovely starter is the veal tartare with artichokes and truffles. They have a veal tenderloin marinated in lime served with an au gratin of zucchini that melts in your mouth; also braised veal cheeks that are sublime. They have two risottos that are standouts: the one with the Maine lobster and the one with black truffles. Superior. The lunch menu is very abbreviated. Here, splurge on dinner, even if you might get treated like the ultimate Outsider.

ESTIATORIO MILOS BY COSTAS SPILIADIS

730 First St., Miami Beach
305-604-6800
www.estiatoriomilos.com
CUISINE: Greek, Seafood
DRINKS: Full Bar
SERVING: Lunch, Dinner
PRICE RANGE: $$$$

The name alone tells you how "important" they are. When did restaurants become movies, with the director's name above the title? "A Steven Spielberg Eatery." But they do deliver the goods here: incredible choice of seafood shipped in from Morocco, Tunisia, Portugal, Nova Scotia and Greece. Though they have a great selection of meats, you'll want to focus on the seafood here. If you want to savor their excellent food but don't want to pay the bill (this is one of the most expensive places in town), stop in for lunch when they have a prix fixe menu for less than $30. I come here for lunch at least once a month, dinner once a year. Excellent wine list, almost all Greek selections that are light and refreshing. $$$$

JAYA AT SETAI
2001 Collins Ave., Miami Beach
855-923-7899
CUISINE: Contemporary, Indian
DRINKS: Full bar
SERVING: 7am to midnight daily
www.thesetaihotel.com
Just plain excellent. Fine food beautifully served. In a town with several really good Sunday brunches, this one excels. It's not the cheapest, but it may very well be the best.

JUVIA
1111 Lincoln Rd., Miami Beach
305-763-8272
www.juviamiami.com
CUISINE: Asian Fusion, Japanese, Seafood
DRINKS: Full Bar
SERVING: Lunch, Dinner
PRICE RANGE: $$$$
Gorgeous setting with penthouse views of South Beach. Creative menu with dishes like Unagi with chocolate and Binchotan-grilled tenderloin. Dine early for sunset view. There are surprisingly few places where you can get an overview of South Beach. This is one of them. If you're on a budget, go to the bar, enjoy the view and eat somewhere else. Shake Shack's in the same building.) Order a beer, which will cost less than a glass of wine and last longer.

KATSUYA BY STARCK
SLS Hotel
1701 Collins Ave., Miami Beach
305-455-2995
www.sbe.com/katsuya/south-beach
CUISINE: Sushi
DRINKS: Full Bar
SERVING: Dinner
PRICE RANGE: $$$$
A chic two-level sushi restaurant in South Beach's new SLS Hotel with a menu of small starters, sushi, robata and other hot dishes. Extensive list of sake and specialty cocktails.

LT STEAK & SEAFOOD

LT STEAK & SEAFOOD

The Betsy Hotel, 1440 Ocean Dr.; Miami Beach
305-673-0044
www.thebetsyhotel.com/dining
CUISINE: Steaks-some seafood
DRINKS: Full bar
SERVING: Breakfast, lunch & dinner daily

Chef Laurent Tourondel's entry in the South Beach restaurant sweepstakes. Not just the steaks for which he's famous, but Dover sole and other seafood specialties as well. Breakfast for two can $60. A recent dinner for four cost over $500. So... make it a special occasion, because it IS special. Extremely talented and attentive waiters. (The best bacon in the world if you have a chance to breakfast here. Worth a special trip for the bacon and scones in the morning.

MR. CHOW

W South Beach Hotel
2201 Collins Ave., 305-695-1695
www.mrchow.com
CUISINE: Chinese
DRINKS: Full bar
SERVING: Dinner nightly

The food's very nice, as a rule, but of course it ought to be. Can't go wrong with the Beijing chicken, the famous green prawns, whatever lobster dish they're serving, and my favorite: the crispy beef and duck. (Oh, and get the fried rice.) They've gone all-out on the décor, and worth a trip just to see the place.

PRIME ONE TWELVE
112 Ocean Dr. (The Browns Hotel), 305-532-8112
www.mylesrestaurantgroup.com
CUISINE: Steakhouse
DRINKS: Full bar
SERVING: Lunch from 11:30 weekdays, dinner from 6:30. Basketball players and other celebs come here to see, be seen, and order the 48 oz. Porterhouse. If you want to go here but not "go there," go for lunch at the bar and order the BLT and a beer. There's an appetizer here, the truffled deviled eggs for $18 that ought to be tried before you die. (In fact, this dish will HELP you die, but you'll go down smiling!)

QUALITY MEATS
1501 Collins Ave, Miami Beach
305-340-3333
www.qualitymeatsmiami.com
CUISINE: Steakhouse/American (New)
DRINKS: Full Bar
SERVING: Dinner
PRICE RANGE: $$$
A Miami location of the famous NYC chophouse, this dining room is located in a historic Art Deco Hotel. Executive chef Craig Koketsu offers a creative menu of classic cuts of beef, not that South Beach needed another steakhouse. Still, this place is a lot of fun—busy, lively, noisy, fun. Menu picks include: Short Ribs and Double tomahawk rib steak. Some items are a little odd: a thick slice of bacon served with peanut butter and a relish including jalapenos. Wow! Most steakhouses carry the same tired old side dishes, but here at Quality Meats, there are some interesting selections, like the creamed corn (out of this world) or the roasted trumpet mushrooms, or the crispy potatoes served in a skillet—when the waiter brings it, he will pour a garlic-herb butter on top. This would make a meal in itself, and one that would be completely satisfying. This place offers a great dining experience with an old world feel.

QUATTRO ITALIANA
1014 Lincoln Rd.; Miami Beach
305-531-4833
www.quattromiami.com
CUISINE: Italian
DRINKS: Full bar
SERVING: lunch and dinner daily
Excellent. Wide range of interesting Italian specialties. Upmarket dining on Lincoln Road. (Go inside and have a look at the stunning bar in the back of the place.)

SMITH & WOLLENSKY

SCARPETTA

Fontainebleau; 4441 Collins Ave., Miami Beach
305-674-4660 / 305-538-2000
www.fontainebleau.com/web/dining/scarpetta
CUISINE: Italian
DRINKS: Full bar
SERVING: Dinner daily from 5:30.
There's no question that when this dowager hotel reopened after a renovation that costs tens of millions of dollars (2010), this was the prize jewel of all the well-hyped restaurants. When you arrive at the hotel, they will have to tell you how to get there, it's so far away from where a cab will drop you. (And I had to stop twice to ask directions.) When you get to the space, you'll find it's just the opposite of what you expected: a small, intimate, charmingly decorated room that feels like it's anywhere but here. The food is nothing short of spectacular. You've never had pasta that was this delicate, unless you've been to Chef Scott Conant's eatery in New York. It's the same great food. Favorite starters are the crispy fritto misto and the creamy polenta. There's also a Japanese mackerel tartar that jumps right out at you. Bypass the steaks, chops and seafood and focus on his pasta dishes as your entrée, especially the scialatelli and the agnolotti dal plin. You'll go nuts. Don't miss the Osso Bucco.

SMITH & WOLLENSKY

1 Washington Ave.; Miami Beach
305-673-2800
www.smithandwollensky.com
CUISINE: American, Steakhouse, Seafood
DRINKS: Full bar
SERVING: lunch and dinner daily

Sorry, but no visit to South Beach is complete without dropping by this place, even if it's for a drink at the outside bar overlooking Gov't Cut where you can see the boat traffic coming into and out of the Port of Miami. They have a cold seafood platter that's killer, and the million-dollar view is free!

VILLA AZUR RESTAURANT & LOUNGE
309 - 23rd St., Miami Beach
305-763-8688
www.villaazurmiami.com
CUISINE: Italian, Mediterranean
DRINKS: Full Bar
SERVING: Dinner
PRICE RANGE: $$$$
Went here on my birthday last year. And immediately returned again and again. A bit of French Riviera elegance in South Beach serving delicious dishes like seared tuna with avocado and baby spinach. Actress Halle Berry's boyfriend is one of the owners. A favorite of celebrities and fashionistas.

SOUTH BEACH
SENSIBLE ALTERNATIVES

I'd say the restaurants in this category are the most "satisfying" on South Beach because they've all achieved unqualified success by delivering really good (and often very fine) food at reasonable prices.

BARCELONETA
1400 20th St, Miami Beach
305-538-9299
www.barcelonetarestaurant.com
CUISINE: Spanish
DRINKS: Full bar
SERVING: Lunch/Dinner
NEIGHBORHOOD: South Beach
Chic storefront eatery with a menu of small plates of typical Spanish fare. Favorites include: Steak tartar and Spicy shrimp. Great wine selection. Great casual dining environment.

BAYSIDE GRILL
The Standard Hotel; 40 Island Ave., Miami Beach 786-245-0880
www.standardhotels.com
CUISINE: Greek, Mediterranean, International
DRINKS: Full bar
SERVING: Daily 7am-midnight
PRICE RANGE: $$$
There are damn few places where you can have a drink and see Biscayne Bay. (Even on Ocean Drive, the park is between you and the water and you can't see the ocean, either, except way out.) Well, over here on the first island on the Venetian Causeway,

you'll find a perfect spot. It's got a pool, a restaurant, a spa. L.A. hotelier Andre Balazs bought the rundown Lido Spa and renovated it into one of his hip Standard hotels. It's just stunning at sunset by the pool. (The French fries are the best!) Note: there's nowhere to park, so you have to valet if you drive. Take a cab.

BODEGA TAQUERIA Y TEQUILA
1220 16th St, Miami Beach
305-704-2145
www.bodegasouthbeach.com
CUISINE: Mexican
DRINKS: Full Bar
SERVING: Lunch & Dinner
PRICE RANGE: $$
This local's favorite serves over-the-top Mexican street food and features a taco truck inside. Great choice for lunch or late-night munching. The real star of this place is the hidden bar.

BYBLOS
1545 Collins Ave, Miami Beach
305-508-5041
www.byblosmiami.com
CUISINE: Mediterranean / Middle Eastern
DRINKS: Full bar
SERVING: Dinner
PRICE RANGE: $$$
This place offers a great dining experience in a plush atmosphere that makes you imagine what Nikki Beach might look like in Greece. (Or anywhere else out there.) High ceilings, lush booths, pillows, divans, lounges. The cuisine is a mishmash of items from Jordan, Israel, Lebanon. All very tasty and very expertly prepared. This place opened after the Canadian owners had a big success with a Byblos in Toronto. Unlike a lot of other upmarket restaurants flooding into Miami, this one is not pretentious and full of itself. Even if you don't like Lamb Ribs, I urge you to get it as a starter. They marinate them 24 hours before they get a rubbing of molasses. Then the ribs are plunked into a blend of Eastern spices & crushed nuts and seeds (called dukka) that results in a crunchy texture to the finished product. Anyway, they are really good. There are numerous delicious dishes like Duck Kibbeh, Eggplant Dumplings and Jeweled Rice. If you know someone who knows this kind of food, treat them to dinner here—they'll help you order. Otherwise, trust the very friendly staff. The wine list is more expensive than it ought to be, so order wisely. Or drink beer, as I do, even better.

THE CAFÉ AT BOOKS & BOOKS
927 Lincoln Rd.; Miami Beach
305-695-8898

www.thecafeatbooksandbooks.com
CUISINE: Contemporary, Eclectic; some good Cuban
DRINKS: Beer & Wine
SERVING: Breakfast, lunch and dinner daily
Take a minute to look up at the historic Sterling Building in which this café is housed. It's one of the best examples of "Streamline Moderne" Art Deco architecture in the country. I used to have an office in this building and loved walking to work there every day. Excellent spot for breakfast, lunch or dinner on Lincoln Road, which you may consider a big fat Tourist Trap with a bunch of overpriced eateries with boring food served indifferently.

CARA MIA TRATTORIA
1040 Alton Rd., Miami Beach
305-397-8624
www.caramiatrattoriasobe.com/
CUISINE: Italian
DRINKS: Beer & Wine
SERVING: lunch / dinner / brunch weekends; prix fixe lunch for $20; prix fixe dinner for $33.
Every time I drove by this place, I thought the sign outside said "Casa Mia," and I thought. "Great. Another Cuban restaurant in South Beach." (Not that there are any more; except for Puerto Sagua, they've all been driven over to Miami by the high rents.) However, it's completely, and wonderfully, Italian. A perfect neighborhood finds that locals love. Unadorned wooden tables (like you might see in a convent) fill the darkened and very lovely room giving off a charming atmosphere. A long bar is inviting for singles or couples. One night I had a starter that involved scallops buried in a little bird's nest of angel hair pasta and then deep-fried. Wow! The fettuccini with the duck ragout a constant standout. Also a braised lamb shank over pasta, another winner. Go for the lemon ricotta cheesecake for dessert—very light. $$$

CIBO WINE BAR
200 South Pointe Dr., Miami Beach, 305-987-6060
www.cibowinebar.com
CUISINE: Italian/Wine Bar
DRINKS: Full Bar
SERVING: Dinner & Weekend Brunch
PRICE RANGE: $$$
Popular new Italian eatery offering a bit of old world charm mixed with a modern industrial twist in terms of its over-the-top and somewhat gaudy décor. If you're not bowled over by the cavernous dining room space, head on up to the large rooftop patio and you will be bowled over. Down in the SoFi section of South Beach, you'll get a great view up here. The menu features classic Italian fare and an impressive list of wines (3,500 bottles).

CLEO SOUTH BEACH
1776 Collins Ave, Miami Beach
305-534-2536
www.sbe.com/cleosouthbeach
CUISINE: Mediterranean/Middle Eastern
DRINKS: Full Bar
SERVING: Dinner
PRICE RANGE: $$$
Located in the hip Redbury Hotel, this modern eatery offers a nice menu of creative Eastern Mediterranean fare. The owners came in from L.A. to launch this place and they brought an extremely competent staff to get things rolling. A very welcoming atmosphere. Menu picks include: Grilled octopus and Tuna Tartare. Nice large bar, which is where you'll find me chatting with the bartender, who makes a powerfully effective Manhattan with Makers Mark.

COCO BAMBU
955 Alton Rd, Miami Beach
786-348-0770
www.cocobambu.com
CUISINE: Brazilian/Seafood
DRINKS: Full Bar
SERVING: Lunch & Dinner
PRICE RANGE: $$$
NEIGHBORHOOD: South Beach
Contemporary multi-level eatery offering a menu of Brazilian seafood plates. This restaurant is part of a Brazilian chain but has a local feel. Still, the place is HUGE. It has some 450 seats, but I've seen their restaurants in Brazil with up to 1,000 seats. The multi-level design breaks it up into smaller rooms so you don't feel so overwhelmed. The large menu of over 100 items matches the size of the place. Sharing is part of the idea here, so don't let the prices get to you that much. There will be enough for 2. Shellfish and fish are the main emphasis here. Favorites: Paella with seafood & lobster and Skirt Steak with fried rice, Coco Bambu Shrimp and Crab cake appetizer. Try the Brazilian beer and Lava Cake. (Or my favorite, the warm banana bread pudding.)

DECK SIXTEEN
1600 Collins Ave, Miami Beach
305-695-7400
https://southbeachmiami.centric.hyatt.com
CUISINE: Spanish / Mediterranean
DRINKS: Full bar
SERVING: Dinner nightly
PRICE RANGE: $$
Located on third floor of Hyatt Centric hotel, offering a menu of Spanish-Mediterranean fare. Chef William Milian's creative menu includes favorites like: Octopus with Giant Beans and Chorizo with little potatoes. Indoor/outdoor seating.

DORAKU
1104 Lincoln Rd., Miami Beach
305-695-8383
www.dorakusushi.com
CUISINE: Japanese/Sushi.
DRINKS: Full bar; SERVING: lunch and dinner daily
Among the dozen places on Lincoln Road where you can get sushi (and I've eaten in all of them multiple times because that's my job), this is the one I always come back to when I'm not forced by work to go elsewhere. (Has one of the few lively bar scenes among Lincoln Road restaurants and a nice if unpublicized Happy Hour good for food as well as drinks.) $$$

DRUNKEN DRAGON
1424 Alton Rd, Miami Beach
305-397-8556
www.drunkendragon.com
CUISINE: Asian Fusion / Korean
DRINKS: Full Bar
SERVING: Dinner
PRICE RANGE: $$
This exceedingly popular Korean eatery featuring Asian Fusion and BBQ took over an old Cuban market and never bothered changing the nondescript big red sign out front that reads, simply enough, MARKET. And for some reason, it's wildly popular, so much so you'll need to book ahead. South Beach's first Korean barbecue restaurant offers tableside grilling and modern Asian tapas. Vegetarian and meat options. Tiki-themed cocktails.

THE DUTCH
W South Beach
2201 Collins Ave., Miami Beach
305-938-3111
www.thedutchmiami.com
CUISINE: American
DRINKS: Full Bar
SERVING: Breakfast-Lunch-Dinner
PRICE RANGE: $$$
Brick walls painted white and shelves holding jars of pickles highlighted by a bold bare lighting design give the place a cozier feel than the ultra trendy swank hotel it's located in. New York Chef Andrew Carmellini brings his more American menu to South Beach instead of his strong Italian menu. The raw bar features 3 or 4 types of oysters any given day. The octopus is slow-cooked and enhanced with paprika. There's a Korean style fried chicken sandwich on the lunch menu that's a surprise. Pappardelle with lamb ragu and sheep's milk ricotta is mouthwatering. Jamaican jerk chicken and steamed red snapper round out an excellent menu. (The wine list is not as rapaciously priced as those in other big-name hotels, so there's another plus.)

FOGO DE CHAO
836 First St., Miami Beach
305-672-0011
www.fogodechao.com
CUISINE: Brazilian Steakhouse.
DRINKS: Full bar
SERVING: lunch weekdays; dinner nightly
Great experience. Massive salad bar comes with your meal (which is prix fixe, and it's all you can eat). Waiters carrying swords with grilled meat move table-to-table supplying you with an endless amount of different kinds of meat. If you're from the middle of nowhere, this is a must. They won't have this in your town. (I'm just glad they have it in this town!) Excellent and reasonable wine list and the most attentive staff. (It's a little heavy for lunch, so if you come for lunch, make this your big meal of the day.) $$

FORTE DEI MARMI
150 Ocean Dr, Miami Beach,786-276-3095
www.fdmmiami.com
CUISINE: Italian/Seafood
DRINKS: Full Bar
SERVING: Dinner, Sunday Brunch
PRICE RANGE: $$$
NEIGHBORHOOD: South Beach
Chic eatery offering a creative menu of Italian classics in a lovely setting. Pink bougainvillea hangs from the arched entrance. Favorites: Linguine Alla Nerano and Calamari Tagliatelle. Great place for Sunday Brunch. If you're having dessert you must try the Sicilian's Pistachio Crème Brulee, an interesting version of crème brulee served with chocolate gelato. All-Italian wine list.

JOE'S STONE CRAB
11 Washington Ave., Miami Beach
305-673-0365
www.joesstonecrab.com
CUISINE: American, Seafood
DRINKS: Full bar
SERVING: lunch, dinner daily October-May; summer hours vary
PRICE RANGE: $$$
The most famous restaurant on South Beach. Opened in 1913, they still serve up great stone crabs. If you don't like stone crabs (I actually met someone who didn't!), order anything on their menu. It's all great. You can even get half a friend chicken for $6.95, some of the best fried chicken you've ever had. If you've never been here before, this is a must. But it's much easier at lunch than dinner to get in. If you have to go to dinner, go early, around 6, and getting in won't be a problem. Later than that, expect a wait of an hour or two. (A great

JOE'S STONE CRAB

place to eat at the bar if you're alone or a couple.) No reservations.

JOE'S TAKEAWAY
11 Washington Ave., Miami Beach
305-673-4611
www.joesstonecrab.com
CUISINE: American
DRINKS: Beer & Wine
SERVING: breakfast, lunch, dinner daily; closed in summer
They even serve breakfast (I have breakfast here 3 times a week when I am in town), and things here are cheaper than you think. There are dozens of restaurants on South Beach that charge more than Joe's for inferior quality food and service. (Try their fried chicken—you get a half-chicken for an astounding $6.95.) $$

LA MODERNA
1874 Bay Rd, Miami Beach
786-717-7274
www.lamoderna-miami.com
CUISINE: Italian / Pizza
DRINKS: Full bar
SERVING: Lunch & Dinner
PRICE RANGE: $$
Trattoria offering a creative menu of Neapolitan pies and rustic-modern pastas. Menu picks include: Spaghetti with caviar and Oyster and crispy leeks. Great creative craft cocktails.

LURE FISHBAR
1601 Collins Ave, Miami Beach
305-695-4550
Loews Hotel
www.lurefishbar.com
CUISINE: Seafood/Sushi
DRINKS: Full bar
SERVING: Dinner
PRICE RANGE: $$$
NEIGHBORHOOD: South Beach
Located in the Loews Hotel, everything is nautical-themed from the décor to the cocktails. Classic seafood menu offering great surf 'n' turf, sushi, and oysters. Try their tasty signature crafted cocktails (most have at least six ingredients). Save room for their delicious Key Lime Pie made with house-made Graham Cracker and roasted white chocolate.

MACALUSO'S ITALIAN CUISINE
1747 Alton Rd., Miami Beach
305-604-1811
www.macalusosmiami.com
CUISINE: Italian American
DRINKS: Beer & Wine
SERVING: Tuesday-Sunday dinner from 6
Just a couple of blocks north of Lincoln Road tucked inside a little strip of stores is one of the best-kept secrets for lovers of Italian food. (Whatever you do, try the meatballs!) This is one of actor Mickey Rourke's favorite haunts when he's in town, as he often is. No reservations accepted. $$$

MACCHIALINA TAVERNA RUSTICA
820 Alton Rd., Miami Beach
305-534-2124
www.macchialina.com
CUISINE: Italian
DRINKS: Full bar
SERVING: Dinner
This intimate (60 seats) eatery serves top-notch Italian fare including great dishes like Eggplant & Mozzarella and Wagyu Carpaccio. While the food is undeniably good, everything on the menu is $10 less at Oliver's just around the corner. (Of course, the food at Oliver's is a peg or two down in quality than this gourmet place.) And the wine list here is not very friendly. I don't remember a single bottle under $50. Not cool. I go to Oliver's 3 times a week, only 3 times a year here. The vibe here, though, is one of the coolest in town. And trust me, it's ALWAYS packed. When I go (OK, maybe it's more than 3 times a year), I arrive promptly when they open at 6 so I can grab a seat and eat at the bar. $$$

MARE MIO
447 Espanola Way, Miami Beach
305-397-8950
www.maremiorestaurant.com
CUISINE: Seafood
DRINKS: Full Bar
SERVING: Lunch & Dinner
PRICE RANGE: $$
NEIGHBORHOOD: South Beach
Located on the historic Spanish street, this cute little eatery offers a creative seafood centric menu. Favorites: Grilled cuttlefish & black ink risotto and Seafood linguini. Fish is very fresh here.

MATADOR ROOM
Edition Hotel
2901 Collins Ave, Miami Beach
786-257-4600
www.matadorroom.com
CUISINE: Spanish/Caribbean
DRINKS: Full Bar
SERVING: Dinner, Late Night
PRICE RANGE: $$$
This upscale eatery offers Jean-Georges Vongerichten's take on Latin cuisine, with some dishes copied from the chef's ABC Cocina in New York. Here you can dine on a seasonal menu of small and large plates. Beautiful oval dining room and bar that overlooks the pool. Menu picks include: Grilled Octopus and Short Ribs. Creative cocktails. The best thing about this place is that it's located off the stunning hotel lobby. I hadn't expected all that white marble. The way they up-lighted the potted palm to get the fronds to cast muted shadows on the white ceiling gave the place a very modern take on a noir look from the 1930s or '40s. Superior design concept, I must say. The hotel bar is expensive and boring, to my taste, and the restaurant also is stuffy and shrug-inducing, requiring an effort. On the weekends, the place is packed as party-goers head to the Basement nightclub downstairs.

MONTY'S SUNSET
300 Alton Rd, Miami Beach
305-672-1148
www.montyssobe.com
CUISINE: Seafood
DRINKS: Full Bar
SERVING: Lunch & Dinner
PRICE RANGE: $$
NEIGHBORHOOD: South Beach
This is about the only place you can go for lunch and use the pool. It's right on the water facing the Third Street Marina, so you get to see all the boats tied up on the docks. Large outdoor tiki hut bar attracts a big crowd. Popular waterfront seafood eatery with a raw bar & the usual

fish shack fare. Besides the Stone crabs this place features live music, DJs, TVs for sports and happy hour special. Favorites: Lobster bisque, grouper tacos and Fried Shrimp. Another plus is the Free Parking – a rarity on South Beach.

NAIYARA
1854 Bay Rd, Miami Beach
786-275-6005
www.naiyara.com
CUISINE: Thai/Japanese
DRINKS: Full bar
SERVING: Dinner
PRICE RANGE: $$$
NEIGHBORHOOD: Miami Beach
Popular eatery serving up a creative menu of Thai street food, sushi and Asian specialties. Favorites include: Crispy bok choy, Chicken dumplings, and Creamy ramen noodle soup with prawns. Unique cocktails. Reservations recommended.

NAUTILUS CABANA CLUB
Nautilus Hotel
1825 Collins Ave, Miami Beach
786-483-2650
www.sixtyhotels.com/nautilus
CUISINE: Latin American
DRINKS: Full Bar
SERVING: Breakfast, Lunch & Dinner
PRICE RANGE: $$
NEIGHBORHOOD: South Beach
Beachside eatery with a menu of seafood-focused Mediterranean fare & vegetarian options. Favorites: Steak and fish, Tzatziki and vegetables. Live Cuban Band. Great choice for Brunch.

NEWS CAFE
800 Ocean Dr., Miami Beach
305-538-6397
www.newscafe.com
CUISINE: American, Middle Eastern;
DRINKS: Full bar
SERVING: 24 hours
PRICE RANGE: $$
Wide variety of American and some Mediterranean dishes. Yep, this is the place Versace had breakfast before being shot. You can, too! (Have breakfast, that is.)

OLIVER'S BISTRO
959 West Ave., Miami Beach
305-535-3050
www.oliversmiamibeach.com

CUISINE: American (some Italian)
DRINKS: Full bar
SERVING: breakfast, lunch & dinner daily. (Opens at 9)
One of the nicest places frequented by locals. Staff is courteous, the food superior, and their excellent chef, Ed Malloy, hasn't allowed the kitchen to fall off the high standards he set when they first opened. In good weather, you can sit outside and watch the locals stroll by on West Avenue.

Starters: We like the Shrimp & Brie Quesadilla, enhanced with sour cream, black bean relish, salsa and the expected guacamole. Yum. Also, we favor the Smoked Salmon & Brie Crostini. Full range of salads, from Crunchy Chicken to a very nice Cobb; Greek Salad with Grilled Calamari; Spicy Beef Salad. A lovely Rare Seared Sushi Grade Ahi Tuna Niciose Salad is a winner, too.

Main course favorites: quite a few pasta and risotto dishes stand out, from as simple as you can get (Linguini Aglio e Olio or Spaghetti & Meatballs). Steak frites platter is good. One of my favorite things here is to order the mussels with spicy sausage in a tomato garlic broth and have them toss a side of pasta into it: for about $20 you get a great meal, half of which you can take home. (They use Italian sausage in the dish instead of the chorizo you get everywhere else in town, making the dish much, much more flavorful.)

Serves "late breakfast" till 2:30 daily, and has a full brunch menu on weekends. Also has a very nice Vegetable Plate. $$$

PUBBELLY
1418 20th St., Miami Beach
305-532-7555
www.pubbelly.com
CUISINE: American, Tapas/Small Plates, Gastro-pub
DRINKS: Beer & Wine
SERVING: Dinner
PRICE RANGE: $$$
A tavern-like restaurant focusing on pork dishes over in the increasingly hip Sunset Harbour area. Pubbelly really launched the scene here when they opened in 2010. Has great energy. Also serving Asian-style tapas and dumplings (stuffed with surprisingly pleasant combinations like duck & pumpkin or pastrami & sauerkraut—I always get some dumplings when I dine here). Delicious food, great service. Go early or expect a wait. (A few seats at the bar where you can squeeze in if you're lucky.)

SARDINIA-ENOTECA RISTORANTE
1801 Purdy Ave., Miami Beach
305-531-2228
www.sardinia-ristorante.com
CUISINE: Italian-Sardinian.

DRINKS: Full bar
SERVING: Daily noon – midnight
PRICE RANGE: $$$
Look over the menu online. This is Sardinian, not Italian. I love the little cheese and meat boards where they let you mix and match cheeses with meats. The side dishes (roasted beets, braised baby Brussels sprouts) are great. My favorite starter is sautéed chicken livers with fava beans. A meal by itself. (The wines are from Sardinia too, but tend to be lighter than the best Italian wines, but they're eminently quaffable.)

SEGAFREDO ESPRESSO
1040 Lincoln Rd., Miami Beach
305-673-0047
http://www.sze-originale.com/
CUISINE: Café, Appetizers
DRINKS: Full bar
SERVING: lunch & dinner daily
PRICE RANGE: $$$
The aim here is to reflect the lifestyle of Italy's famously fun and charming coffee bars. It's hard to beat the ambience here – lounging on a sofa out on Lincoln Road with a coffee or a drink or a meal. (The fountain is by famed Cuban artist Carlos Alves.)

SPIGA
1228 Collins Ave, Miami Beach
305-534-0079
www.spigarestaurant.com
CUISINE: Italian / Seafood
DRINKS: Beer & Wine Only
SERVING: Dinner
PRICE RANGE: $$$
I tend to forget about this intimate eatery offers a menu of Northern Italian cuisine including great seafood and homemade pastas. Why? Because it's tucked inside the lobby of the tiny and elegant Impala Hotel. It's been here for years and I just love it. Outdoor garden dining. Nice wine list.

STILTSVILLE FISH BAR
1787 Purdy Ave, Miami Beach
786-353-0477
www.stiltsvillefishbar.com
CUISINE: Seafood, Tapas/Small Plates, Cocktail Bars
DRINKS: Full Bar
SERVING: Dinner, Lunch & Dinner Sat - Sun
PRICE RANGE: $$$
NEIGHBORHOOD: Miami Beach
Casual eatery featuring big open garage style window/doors. It's a lot less hectic and bustling during the week, while on weekends, it's one of "the" places to be. Without a reservation on the weekends, you'll get turned away. As "rustic" as they've tried to make this place, there's nothing rustic about the food. It's smart, sophisticated, expertly prepared—everything. Creative menu offering fresh

STILTSVILLE FISH BAR

options from fish to vegetables. The fish is delivered daily from fishermen working in Key Largo, Key West and here in Miami. Very fish-centric menu. The leftover fish parts are smoked to make a very nice dip which you ought to get as a starter for the whole table to sample. A popular dish is the whole fried snapper. (Don't worry about forgetting this—the waiters push it, actually.) It's visually striking when it lands on your table. Impressive salads. Favorites: Shrimp 'N Grits and Lobster Mac N' Mushrooms. The chef is noted for his fried chicken (which he debuted at Yardbird over near Lincoln Road). But don't get it—it's far too expensive. (Instead, get the fried chicken next time you're at Joe's Stone Crab—you'll get a half chicken for what it costs for a single piece here.) Dining room includes bar (with perhaps the most uncomfortable bar stools in all Christendom) and lounge area.

STUBBORN SEED
101 Washington Ave, Miami Beach
786-322-5211
www.stubbornseed.com
CUISINE: American (New)/Seafood
DRINKS: Full Bar
SERVING: Dinner; closed Mondays
PRICE RANGE: $$$
NEIGHBORHOOD: South Beach
Opened by Top Chef 13 winner Jeremy Ford. This very small eatery offers a menu of seasonal American cuisine created by a master at his craft. Tip: Try the Chef's Tasting Menu which has some of the menu's best. Favorites: Smoked foie gras,

Maine Lobster poached in butter, lavash (chicken liver butter), warm celery root, and the Slow Cooked Florida Snapper. Craft cocktails. I hope to God this place stays open more than a year. I almost skipped putting this place in my book because so many of this "type" of place never make it. The food is so good I am praying. Yes, the portions are small and the prices are steep, but still… this place is a superior achievement. I don't think the name helps, but as long as he keeps cooking the way he's cooking, I don't give a damn what he calls it.

SUGAR FACTORY
Hotel Victor, 1144 Ocean Dr., Miami Beach; 305-604-0323
www.sugarfactory.com/miami
CUISINE: American (New) / Desserts
DRINKS: Full bar
SERVING: Breakfast, Lunch & Dinner
PRICE RANGE: $$
Located in the beautiful art deco Hotel Victor, this newly-redecorated 3,000 square foot brasserie offers a candy shop up front and patio dining overlooking Ocean Drive and the ocean. Known for their world-famous Couture Pops, creative cocktails, the menu also offers pancakes, crepes, salads, burgers, and creative desserts.

SWEET LIBERTY DRINKS & SUPPLY COMPANY
237-B 20th St, Miami Beach
305-763-8217
www.mysweetliberty.com
CUISINE: American (New)
DRINKS: Beer & Wine Only
SERVING: Dinner, Brunch on Sundays
PRICE RANGE: $$
NEIGHBORHOOD: South Beach
Near the Bass Museum and the renovated Convention Center is this hideaway known and frequented by every serious bartender in Miami because it (well, the boss Lermayer) gets credit for spawning the "craft cocktail" trend in Miami. The bartenders here really know their shit. It's very unassuming, even down market, but they have cheap oysters during happy hour, and VERY reasonable prices for food. (Cocktails are not outrageously priced.) Favorites: Lobster rolls, fried chicken and Cauliflower nachos. Happy hour specials. A pool table for those interested. Lermayer says, "The cocktail is America's first epicurean contribution to the world." And unlike all those other places where they serve "craft cocktails," here you'll find no velvet rope and (for Miami) a refreshing absence of bullshit and attitude.

TANUKI
1080 Alton Rd, Miami Beach
305-615-1055
www.tanukimiami.com
CUISINE: Asian Fusion, Dim Sum, Japanese
DRINKS: Full Bar
SERVING: Dinner only on Monday & Tues, Lunch & Dinner Wed - Sun
PRICE RANGE: $$$
NEIGHBORHOOD: Miami Beach
Upscale eatery specializing in sushi, dim sum and wok with some of the finest Japanese, Thai, Korean, Malaysian and Chinese dishes. Favorites: Dim sum and Shanghainese soup dumplings. For a special occasion try their Peking Duck. Great desserts.

TAP TAP
819 5th St., Miami Beach
305-672-2898
www.taptapmiamibeach.com
CUISINE: Haitian; Caribbean
DRINKS: Full bar
SERVING: Dinner nightly
If you've never had Haitian food, try this mainstay and you won't have to cross the Causeway to go to Little Haiti. Stewed goat is one of my favorites. Or the whole red snapper fried and served with flair. This food is wonderful and exciting. Besides the food, you get to surround yourself with Haitian art. Murals on the walls are colorfully alive in that distinctive Haitian style and there are numerous individual pieces as well. $$-$$$

UPLAND MIAMI
49 Collins Ave, Miami Beach
305-602-9998
www.uplandmiami.com
CUISINE: American (New)
DRINKS: Beer & Wine Only
SERVING: Dinner, Lunch Sat & Sun
PRICE RANGE: $$$
NEIGHBORHOOD: South Beach
This chic NYC spin-off with fine dining is just a block from the beach, but it's sophisticated and casual at the same time. Bright and cheerful place. It offers a creative menu of wood-fired dishes with Californian & Italian influences. Favorites: Salmon, Wood roasted beets, wood fired Florida prawns, dry-aged bone-in New York strip and Tuscan-Style Lamb Chops. I always get the crispy squash blossoms to start. Bartenders are well trained, too. Nice wine selection. Has a bar with 6 or 7 seats where you can eat if you're by yourself. Chef Justin Smillie comes from Upland, Calif., which explains the name of this place.

VIA EMILIA 9
1120 15th St., Miami Beach
786-216-7150
www.viaemilia9.com
CUISINE: Italian
DRINKS: Beer & Wine Only
SERVING: Lunch & Dinner
PRICE RANGE: $$
NEIGHBORHOOD: South Beach
This is one of those little "finds" you read guidebooks like this to discover. You'd never stumble onto it by yourself. Just a half-block east of Alton Road is this Italian eatery with a menu of authentic Italian classics and house made Perezpasta. You'll see the Chef Wendy Cacciatori behind the counter cooking almost every night. The place is split into 2 rooms, a diner-counter on one side (behind which he cooks) and am intimate, charming romantic room on the other side of the wall where candlelight flickers on the little tables. (I prefer to sit in the brighter diner side just because I love to watch this guy cook.) His concept was simple when he came to South Beach—he'd only cook dishes you could get on the via Emilia in Italy that happens to run through towns like Bologna, Parma and Modena. If you can't get to Italy anytime soon, you're in luck. Come here. Favorites: Eggplant parmigiana and gnocchi. Well, any of the pastas. They're all great. Nice wine list. Reservations recommended on weekends, when it fills with locals.

SOUTH BEACH
QUALITY BARGAIN SPOTS

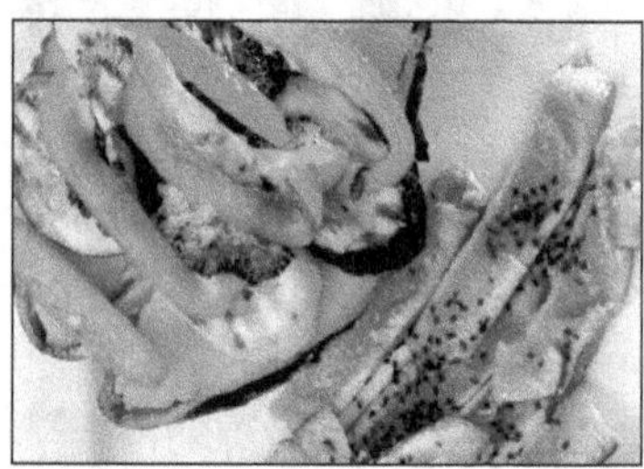

APPLE A DAY
1534 Alton Rd., Miami Beach
305-538-4569
www.appleadaymiami.com
CUISINE: Juice bar/Smoothies
DRINKS: No Booze
SERVING: 8 a.m. – 10 p.m.
PRICE RANGE: $$
NEIGHBORHOOD: South Beach
Health food market offering usual health food items plus fresh juices, salads, and wraps. Favorites: Vegan pizza and variety of tacos. Raw vitamins and supplements. Counter-service with seating indoors & out.

BIG PINK
157 Collins Ave., Miami Beach
305-532-4700
305-531-0888 for delivery.
http://www.mylesrestaurantgroup.com/
CUISINE: American, Diner

DRINKS: Full bar
SERVING: Breakfast, lunch and dinner from 8am.
PRICE RANGE: $$
TVs for sports fans. You'd never know it to walk in this joint, but the same guy who owns Prime 112 a couple of blocks away owns this place slinging out chicken wings and draft beer for pennies on the dollar compared to the higher-profile place. Really good American diner food.

BOLIVAR
841 Washington Ave., Miami Beach:
305-305-0801
www.bolivarmiamibeach.com
CUISINE: Peruvian, Colombian, Venezuelan
DRINKS: Full Bar
SERVING: Lunch, Dinner
Classic South American dishes served. Delicious menu items include salmon in Creole sauce with cilantro rice. Romantic atmosphere and excellent service. $$

CARROT EXPRESS
1755 Alton Rd., Miami Beach
305-535-1379
www.carrotexpressmiamibeachfl.com
CUISINE: Vegetarian/Juice Bar
DRINKS: No Booze
SERVING: 10 a.m. – 9 p.m.
PRICE RANGE: $$
NEIGHBORHOOD: South Beach
Counter-service spot offering a menu of vegan & vegetarian fare. Favorites: Chicken melt on pita and Tuna wrap. Great smoothies.

CHALAN ON THE BEACH
1580 Washington Ave., Miami Beach
305-532-8880 No web site
CUISINE: Peruvian
DRINKS: Beer & wine
SERVING: Lunch and dinner daily
It looks like a trashy dump on the outside, but once you slide indoors, you can expect some of the best Peruvian food to be had in Miami. And cheap, too. No other Latin America culture prepares seafood as well as Peruvians, in my view. If you're not familiar with this cuisine, the menu will dazzle you. $$

CHEESEBURGER BABY

1505 Washington Ave., Miami Beach
305-531-7300
www.cheeseburgerbaby.net
CUISINE: the great American burger
DRINKS: beer & wine
SERVING: lunch and dinner daily. Free delivery day and night
There's been a proliferation of burger joints on South Beach in the last couple of years, but these are without question the JUICIEST BURGERS in South Beach. There's a great lunch special: ½ lb. cheeseburger with French fries and a 16 oz. soda, including free refills, $6.99. Try to beat this deal anywhere else. All beef is certified Angus. The place is really a dive, and the air conditioning is a little iffy, but if you don't mind sitting at a counter, stop here. $

DAVID'S CAFÉ CAFECITO

919 Alton Rd., Miami Beach
305-534-8736
www.davidscafecafecito.com
CUISINE: Cuban
DRINKS: Beer & Wine
SERVING: Breakfast / Lunch / Dinner (6 am to 10 pm)
PRICE RANGE: $
This is my go-to place when I get that urgent need for Cuban food, which in Miami means 3 or 4 times a week! For decades this café was a fixture in locations on Collins Avenue and Lincoln Road, but soaring rents pushed them out of Lincoln Road. Unlike a lot of businesses, they didn't move across the Bay to Miami—they found this location on a busy corner of Alton Road. They serve the same traditional Cuban menu they always have: Picadillo; excellent Cuban sandwiches and Cuban steak sandwiches; vaca frita; arroz con pollo, many others. If you're not sure, just try one of the specials that change daily.

LA SANDWICHERIE

229 14 St., Miami Beach
305-532-8934
www.lasandwicherie.com
CUISINE: Sandwiches; French
DRINKS: beer & wine
SERVING: 8 a.m. to 5 a.m.
(till 6 a.m. on weekends)
Whoever figured this place would last for 20 years? I first came across this placed stumbling out of South Beach's oldest (and still the best) dive bar across the street, the Deuce. It's just a little spot, with an outdoor counter and no indoor seating. Nice sandwiches ($6-$9) always served on crunchy baguettes of soft croissants. You can sort of make each sandwich to order. It's like the archetypal Subway, only they wish.

MY CEVICHE
235 Washington Ave., Miami Beach:
305-397-8710
www.myceviche.com
CUISINE: Seafood, Peruvian
DRINKS: No Alcohol
SERVING: Lunch, Dinner
PRICE RANGE: $$
It's a little hole-in-the wall but co-owners Roger Duarte and James Beard Award-nominated chef Sam Gorenstein are serving delicious ceviche. Everybody I know who loves ceviche LOVES this place. Very cheap, too.

PARRILLA LIBERTY & PIZZA
1255 Washington Ave., Miami Beach
305-532-7599
www.laparrillaliberty.com
CUISINE: Argentine
DRINKS: beer & wine
SERVING: Daily noon – midnight
All the favorites from Argentina but cheap, cheap, cheap! (A little more chewy than great meat, but still… don't eat here if you have dentures.) $

PINOCCHIO
760 Ocean Dr., Miami Beach
305-672-3535
CUISINE: Italian deli
DRINKS: beer & wine
SERVING: lunch, dinner daily
PRICE RANGE: $$
Tucked in among the t-shirt shops and other ordinary stores in this area of Ocean Drive are 2 or 3 "finds," places so special they're worth an extra look. This is one of them. The Gigli family owns this fine little Italian deli; they also own a hotel in San Gimignano (Siena). You can "make your own" panini, choosing from an enormous selection of cheeses, meats, toppings. Excellent bruschette and tramezzini. You know you're in the right place when you look around and realize everybody's speaking Italian… except you. (They make their own gelato here.)

UNDER THE MANGO TREE
737 5th St., Miami Beach
786-558-5103
www.mangotreemiami.com
CUISINE: Juice Bars/Smoothies/Acai Bowls

DRINKS: No Booze
SERVING: 8 a.m. – 6 p.m.
PRICE RANGE: $$
NEIGHBORHOOD: South Beach
Small counter-serve juice bar with a selection of veggie snacks and sandwiches. Favorites: Marley Acai Bowl and Spicy Kale Melt. Impressive juice selection. Eco-friendly gift items.

MIDDLE & NORTH BEACHES

(from 30th Street in Miami Beach up through Bal Harbour, Surfside, Aventura) & MIAMI NORTH

This section includes everything in the County north from (and including) the 79th Street Causeway (on the beach side), the northern part of Miami Beach, the few restaurants on the Causeway; Bal Harbour and Bay Harbor. On the mainland, it includes Miami Shores north to the town of North Miami and the inaccurately named City of North Miami Beach (it has no beach and is a hideous, relentlessly tacky part of this town) up to Aventura, where you'll find a few nice places.

CAFÉ AVANTI
732 – 41st St., Miami Beach
305-538-4400
www.cafeavanti.com
CUISINE: Italian
DRINKS: full bar
SERVING: L weekdays; D nightly.
Frequented by locals who love the food. It's the perfect cozy spot that makes traditional dishes even better than any Italian Grandma. I go there specifically for the linguini con Vongole (they use 2 dozen tender clams in this dish). They also carry the Delaplaine fine sparkling wine from Napa. Save room for the dessert cart. Jessica, the owner's daughter, is the hostess with the mostess. There's plenty of parking on the street and a "private" back door entrance. $$$

CARPACCIO
Bal Harbour Shops, 9700 Collins Ave., Bal Harbour: 305-867-7777
www.carpaccioatbalharbour.com
CUISINE: Italian; DRINKS: full bar;
SERVING: lunch, dinner
I get up here about 3 or 4 times a year. I sit at the bar because at the tables you're surrounded by the "ladies who lunch" crowd who come up here to shop. The hustle and bustle of the place is fun because you feel like you're in New York. (Often, waiters forget to tell you the specials. Ask for them. I almost never order off the menu any more. The specials are always that good.) $$$

THE FORGE

THE FORGE

432 Arthur Godfrey Rd. (41st St.), Miami Beach: 305-538-8533
www.theforge.com

CUISINE: Steakhouse; varied cuisines
DRINKS: full bar
SERVING: dinner nightly.
PRICE RANGE: $$$$

The Forge now styles itself, rather grandly, as The Forge Restaurant – Wine Bar by Shareef Malnik, as if this were a painting. But it doesn't leave any question in your mind who's in charge here.

Shareef has totally reinvented The Forge by completely doing away with the old fustian faux-Victorian, Beaux Arts bordello look his father Alvin instituted when he opened the place in 1968. Now, in lieu of the heavy-handed décor, you've got a light-filled room, the dark mahogany look replaced with blond wall paneling. The place is gorgeous, and still worth a trek up to Middle Beach.

With so many steakhouses proliferating on South Beach, one tends to forget that this was the steakhouse of note for so many decades (aside from the old Embers).

The menu has been updated along with the décor. Most plates feature "locally sourced" ingredients. It's all very nice, from the pastas dishes to the creative salads and the succulent seafood.

Still, my heart still goes for the Forge Super Steak, which they have kept on the menu. Yummy. Still has that world-famous wine cellar.

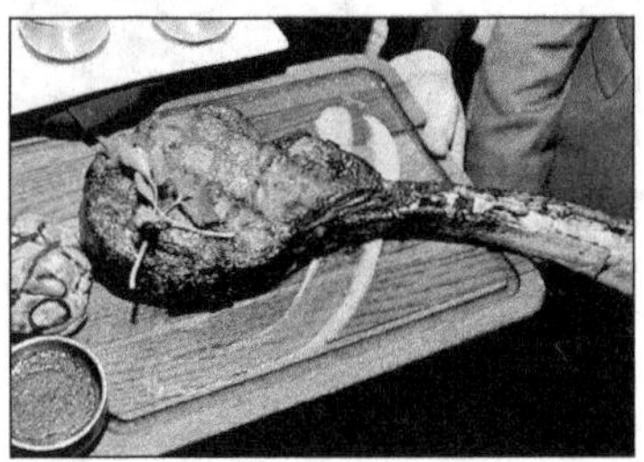

HAKKASAN
Fontainebleau, 4441 Collins Ave., Miami Beach: 786-276-1388
www.hakkasan.com
CUISINE: Chinese
DRINKS: full bar
SERVING: nightly from 6; dim sum lunch weekends, 12-3.
PRICE RANGE: $$$$
I must say that Chinese food has always been Chinese food to me. By that, I mean the concept of "gourmet" Chinese food has similarly seemed to me like a misnomer. But years ago I went to a place in London and then a place down in Miami called Christine Lee's, and my opinion changed instantly. When it's done right, there is no better food than Chinese, and Hakkasan proves the point. Anything you select from the extensive menu will please. But I'm partial to the crisp-skinned roasted duck. I have to have it every trip.

LA CÔTE
Fontainebleau, 4441 Collins Ave., Miami Beach: 305-674-4710
www.fontainebleau.com
CUISINE: American; some European
DRINKS: full bar
SERVING: lunch, early dinner (till 7 p.m.)
Flatbreads, salads, sandwiches. Second floor of the pool deck at this famous hotel. A great place to look over the ocean. Believe it or not, most of the places you can eat in the hotels lining the water don't have water views, obstructed as they are by sand dunes, sea oats, berms, and other manmade obstacles. But here, you're above it all.

LE ZOO
BAL HARBOUR SHOPS
9700 Collins Ave., Bal Harbour
305-602-9663
www.lezoo.com
CUISINE: French
DRINKS: Beer & Wine Only
SERVING: Lunch & Dinner
PRICE RANGE: $$$
NEIGHBORHOOD: Bal Harbour
Popular brasserie with an authentic French feel. It's like sitting on the sidewalk at a Parisian café. Except you're surrounded by the upscale shops like Prada, Chanel and Saks. It's right next door to the old standby that's been in Bal Harbour for decades, Carpaccio. But I always choose this place over Carpaccio. It's located right at the valet, so you're in for a treat if you like to look at expensive cars. Aston Martins, Bugattis, Lamborghinis, Rolls Royces, you name it. There's a small indoor section, but it's more fun to sit outside. Menu of French

classics. Favorites: Veal Piccata and Steak Tartare Du Parc. Though I've had everything on the menu, I gravitate toward the steak frites more often than not. The shoestring fries are expertly cooked. (If they have cucumber soup the day you visit, for God's sake get it. So refreshing and flavorful. I could drink this stuff by the gallon.) Great cocktails and an impressive wine list.

NOBU
4525 Collins Ave., Miami Beach
305-695-3232
www.noburestaurants.com
CUISINE: Japanese
DRINKS: Full bar
SERVING: dinner nightly
South Beach branch of Chef Nobu Matsuhisa's Japanese empire. Among the cold dishes (these are all appetizers), love the yellowtail sashimi with tiny slices of Jalapeno (hot!); salmon kelp roll; sea urchin tiradito; yellowfin tuna tataki; and the monkfish pate with caviar. Standouts among hot starters include their famous rock shrimp tempura; Alaskan king crab tempura; Tasmanian ocean trout with crispy baby spinach. Wide range of Kushiyaki and Tobanyaki specialties as well as the usual sushi and sashimi selections a la carte.

NORMAN'S AMERICAN BAR & GRILL
6770 Collins Ave., Miami Beach
305-868-9248
www.normans.biz
CUISINE: sports bar; gastro pub
DRINKS: full bar
SERVING: Lunch / Dinner daily
Handsome wood paneling highlights this friendly spot in North Beach. Great happy hour with the best prices, pool tables. Sports bars are not noted for the quality of their food, but this one is. The meatball sandwich: three big and hearty meatballs. The burgers, excellent. (Try the onion rings with your burger.) Quesadillas and Philly cheesesteaks also very good. $$

THE PALM
9650 E. Bay Harbor Dr., Bay Harbor Islands: 305-868-7256
CUISINE: steakhouse
DRINKS: full bar
SERVING: dinner from 5
www.thepalm.com
Yes, this is the same Palm as the one in New York. Same menu. Same everything. Still the best steaks anywhere, and all those super side dishes everybody else

has copied. Bay Harbor is reached by going north on Collins Avenue. Take a left at 96th Street and go west over the bridge into the little island town of Bay Harbor. Take the first right. It's there on the left. I remember this place when it was called the Post & Paddock. A great room. Worth a trip. $$$$

DESIGN DISTRICT MIDTOWN WYNWOOD BISCAYNE CORRIDOR

This section includes the hot new restaurant area "Midtown," which is separated from the Design District by 36th Street. To the north of 36th Street is the Design District; to the south, Midtown.

Wynwood is just to the south of Midtown.

The Biscayne Corridor runs from Downtown up along a seedy but slowly improving Biscayne Boulevard until you hit the Miami Shores area, where things die down.

You'll find a lot of cheap restaurants ($ and $$) here because it's not about tourists, it's about locals.

100 MONTADITOS
3252 NE 1st Ave., Miami
305-921-4373 / Midtown
100montaditos.com
CUISINE: Spanish / Sandwiches / Basque
DRINKS: Beer/ Wine
SERVING: Lunch/Dinner
This place is unbelievable. A "montadito" is basically a bite-sized, open-faced 'sandwich' found across Spain's Basque region. They feature tasty ingredients 'mounted' on thick slices of baguette. The 100 refers to the 100 different types of montadito you can order. Pork, fish, chicken, beef, cheese, salty hams, you name it. Each one ranges from $1 to $3. Cheap, cheap, cheap. A lively, fun place to go. (When I lunch there with someone, I'll order 3 montaditos and the other person chooses 3—all with different fillings—and then we cut them in half so we each get 6 small sandwiches.) There's another one of these places on South Beach, 13th Street and Washington Avenue. $

1111 PERUVIAN BISTRO
1111 SW 1st Ave, #106-D, Miami
786-615-9633
www.1111peruvianbistro.com/
CUISINE: Peruvian
DRINKS: Full bar
SERVING: Lunch & Dinner; closed Sun
PRICE RANGE: $$$
NEIGHBORHOOD: Midtown
Sleek modern eatery offering Peruvian specialties with Asian twists. Popular dishes like ceviche, tiraditos, King crab and Poached chicken causa. High quality food.

ALTER

ALTER

223 NW 23rd St., Miami
305-573-5996
www.altermiami.com
CUISINE: American (New)
DRINKS: Full Bar
SERVING: Lunch (till 2:30) & Dinner (from 7) Tues-Sat; closed Sun & Mon.
PRICE RANGE: $$$

Modern new eatery offering a menu of refined and creative New American cuisine. One of the hottest restaurants in all of Miami. No white tablecloths, just plain wooden tables and stark wooden chairs. Very trendy, but don't hold that against the place, because the food pouring out of the open kitchen is most certainly up to snuff. Menu picks include: Rock Shrimp roll; Eggplant "pastrami" (I know what it sounds like, just try it); deboned chicken stuffed with ground up thigh meat & foie gras; luscious prawns served over grits and topped with chorizo oil, mole and huitlacoche cream. (You won't find this kind of "shrimp & grits" in Atlanta or Charleston!) Wonderful place. Very exciting. (But to be completely honest, half the people I bring here hate the place, finding the food presentation to be highly pretentious. You'll get a soup bowl the size of a Frisbee with a tiny little spoonful of soup in it. That sort of thing. Needless to say, the chef has won almost every award you can possibly win.)

BAHAMIAN CONNECTION

4400 NW 2nd Ave., Miami
305-576-6999 / Design District
www.bahamian-connection-grill.com

CUISINE: Bahamian
DRINKS: Beer/Wine
SERVING: Breakfast/Lunch
This joint is definitely off the beaten path and it's in a dumpy, mostly black part of town. But the Bahamian food is great. Try the stew fish, which is fried snapper covered with gravy; the salmon cakes; the "souse," which is chicken or conch boiled till it's soft and then spiced up with limes and peppers. Hell, just get anything on this menu. You'll never have anything like it again. $$

BEAKER & GRAY
2637 N. Miami Ave., Miami
305-699-2637
www.beakerandgray.com
CUISINE: Modern American/Tapas
DRINKS: Full bar
SERVING: Lunch/Dinner; Dinner only on Sat & Sun
PRICE RANGE: $$
NEIGHBORHOOD: Wynwood
This is a cool hot spot near my warehouse (where we keep our wine) and studio (where I write my books). Everybody loves it. The guys here have joined forces to created this innovative eatery offering internationally inspired American fare. While you might have heard of the items on the menu, the way they add their own little twists make everything very distinctive and unique, from the Cuban croquettas to the Chicken fingers, Pumpkin gnocchi and cauliflower. Indoor and outdoor seating.

BLUE COLLAR
6730 Biscayne Blvd., Miami
305-756-0366 / Biscayne Corridor
www.bluecollarmiami.com
CUISINE: American
DRINKS: Beer & Wine
SERVING: Lunch, Dinner, Brunch
One of my favorite places in Miami. Chef Danny Serfer and his talented team, working out of a rundown motel on Biscayne, have created one of the "go-to" places in Miami, frequented by highbrow and lowbrow alike. They dish up American comfort food in a small comfortable setting. Pork & Beans, Shrimp & Grits, Braised Brisket, Chicken Cordon Bleu, all worth ordering. One of the things I like about this place is the blackboard listing about 20 vegetable dishes prepared creatively: you can choose 4 of them for $19. Curried cauliflower, grilled asparagus with a blue cheese vinaigrette, warm potato salad with bacon. You get the idea. A meal by itself. Plan on sharing. Delicious desserts. $$

BUENA VISTA DELI
4590 NE 2nd Ave., Miami
305-576-3945 / Design District

buenavistadeli.com
CUISINE: American
DRINKS: Beer/Wine
SERVING: Breakfast/Lunch
Great bakery & deli on the corner just steps away from Buena Vista Bistro (same owners). Fine sandwiches, simple atmosphere. Check out the pastries. Indoor or outdoor. $

CHARCOAL BAR & GRILL

Wynwood Yard
82 NW 29th St., Miami
786-646-2998
www.charcoalmiami.com
CUISINE: American (Traditional), Bars, Seafood
DRINKS: Full Bar
SERVING: Dinner, Lunch on Sunday, Closed Monday
PRICE RANGE: $$$
NEIGHBORHOOD: Wynwood
Popular new addition to Miami's fast expanding culinary scene. Located in The Wynwood Yard, this full-service eatery has been created from modified shipping containers. Basic menu of locally sourced, off-the-grill seafood, meats and veggies. Menu picks: Grilled scallops & octopus and Duck Breast Steak. Indoor & Outdoor seating.

DELLA TEST KITCHEN

Wynwood Yard
56 NW 29th St., Miami
305-351-2961
www.dellabowls.com
CUISINE: Vegan, Vegetarian, Caribbean
DRINKS: Full Bar
SERVING: Lunch & Dinner
PRICE RANGE: $$
NEIGHBORHOOD: Wynwood
A small, stationary food truck with a patio of picnic tables serving a plant-based menu. Favorite: Caribbean Bowl – black coconut rice, adashah, plantain, avocado, kale, toasted coconut and yellow sauce. All the bowls can be customized. There's usually live music at night.

ENRIQUETA'S SANDWICH SHOP

186 NE 29th St., Miami
305-573-4681 / Wynwood
No web site
CUISINE: Cuban
DRINKS: Beer/Wine
SERVING: Breakfast/Lunch till 3pm.
Really basic Cuban food. Fast, cheap and in the most interesting little spot. (I even put this place in my novel, The Meter Maid

Murders—it's the place where the robbers stop to get a Cuban sandwich and café con leche.) Breakfast: two eggs, bacon or ham, Cuban toast, café con leche, and a cup of fresh squeezed orange juice, is less than McDonald's. Lunch is just as good and just as reasonable. Everybody in Miami has been here at one time or another. Power players from downtown, cops off the street, construction workers, the UPS driver. It's all locals, no tourists. Although Cubans aren't noted for their punctuality, this place closes promptly at 3, but if you get in by 3, you can order and they won't throw you out.

JACK'S HOME COOKING
900 S Miami Ave, Miami
786-452-1932
www.jacksmiami.com
CUISINE: Italian/American Traditional
DRINKS: Full Bar
SERVING: Lunch & Dinner
PRICE RANGE: $$
NEIGHBORHOOD: Downtown
Popular mom-and-pop style eatery offering a menu of Italian classics. Pictures of famous people (and some not so famous), all named Jack, line the walls. Favorites: Meatballs and Chicken Parmesan. I always get the sausages & peppers as a starter, but the pastas are wonderfully tasty, like the Jackie Collins with corkscrew pasta with marinara sauce & cherry tomatoes, basil and mozzarella. The rigatoni has gravy, meatballs, sausage, short ribs and ricotta cheese. After you eat this tasty dish, you'll barely be able to move. Try the Jack Dawson pasta dish with vodka sauce with a perfect dash of truffle. Chocolate torte makes a good dessert choice, if you don't stuff yourself. Owned by long-time South Beach club boys Alan Roth and J.P. Parlavechio. Roth owned a popular club called Rumi back in the day (when my sister Renee and I were in the club business as well). J.P. came down in the early 1990s from New York to pal around with Tommy Pooch, another club man and friend of ours, as well as actor Mickey Rourke. But he never went back home. Now he's cooking dishes taught to him by his mom and grandmother. A welcome addition to the neighborhood. This place has already become an institution. High quality food with reasonable prices in a friendly location. Indoors or outdoors where they've converted the old porch into a wide deck. Great meeting place for friends.

JIMMY'S EASTSIDE DINER
7201 Biscayne Blvd., Miami
305-754-3692 / Biscayne Corridor
No web site
CUISINE: American/Diner
DRINKS: No Bar
SERVING: Breakfast/ Lunch
Although Jimmy's is your typical greasy spoon diner, the food is always really good. This diner has been around for a very long time, a favorite of locals. When

they have it on the menu, try the lamb shank. Delicious. $

JIMMY'Z KITCHEN
2700 N. Miami Ave., Miami
305-573-1505/ Wynwood
jimmyzkitchen.com
CUISINE: American / Puerto Rican
DRINKS: Beer/Wine
SERVING: Lunch/Dinner
Get the "mofongo." This is mashed up plantains onto which you add either chicken beef, pork, whatever, to complete the dish. Fun little place with floor to ceiling windows, bright and airy. (My office is a block away so we go here all the time.) Careful, though. Don't let the plastic chairs and simple décor fool you: this place is pretty expensive for what it is. I usually get the Cobb salad (chicken is cooked to order for each one). $$-$$$

JOEY'S ITALIAN CAFÉ
2506 NW 2nd Ave, Miami
305-438-0488 / Wynwood
www.joeyswynwood.com
CUISINE: Italian
DRINKS: Full Bar
SERVING: Lunch / Dinner
Always a lively crowd in this spot owned by Tony Goldman's son, Joey. Updated modern Italian cuisine. Always fun. $$-$$$

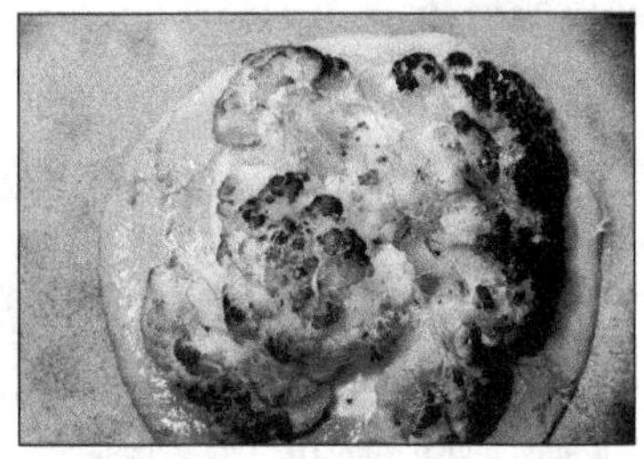

KYU
251 NW 25th St, Miami
786-577-0150
www.kyumiami.com
CUISINE: Asian Fusion
DRINKS: Full bar
SERVING: Lunch & Dinner; closed Mon
PRICE RANGE: $$
NEIGHBORHOOD: Wynwood
Modern hipster eatery with a great menu of Asian fare and creative cocktails. Favorites include: Butter Fried Chicken and Crispy Pork "Guy" (fried pork belly pieces – delicious). Great happy hour menu. Reservations recommended.

MIGNONETTE
210 NE 18th St (corner of 2nd Ave), Miami, 305-374-4635
www.mignonettemiami.com
CUISINE: American; oyster bar; seafood
DRINKS: Beer & Wine
SERVING: Lunch-Dinner-Brunch

NEIGHBORHOOD: Edgewater (just south of Wynwood)
Danny Serfer is famous in these parts for a restaurant further up Biscayne Boulevard, Blue Collar, where American comfort food has never been rendered more comfortably. Here, just 2 blocks off Biscayne, and right across the Causeway from South Beach, he has an oyster bar that also serves a wide variety of fresh seafood (from whole hog snapper to scallop crudo). When I go, I sit at the bar and choose from 10 or more oyster selections while drinking a nice Alsatian pinot blanc. (He's only a few blocks from my office.) I usually avoid things like fried clams on Miami menus. But when I tried them here, I realized he was making these dishes the way they would on Cape Cod. Better, even. Try the fried conch as well.. By the way, across the street is one of the oldest cemeteries in Miami, well worth a stroll through after stuffing yourself here.

MANDOLIN AEGEAN BISTRO
4312 NE 2nd Ave., Miami
305-749-9140/ Design District
mandolinmiami.com
CUISINE: Greek, with some mixed Mediterranean
DRINKS: Beer/Wine
SERVING: Dinner
Intimate and cozy (and we mean intimate—it's in a small house) with great service and great food. Everybody raves about the white sangria, but it's not for me. (Wine for me.) I've tried almost every dish on the menu, and there's not a loser in the lot. Outdoors is nice in good weather. $-$$

MC KITCHEN
4141 NE 2nd Ave., Miami
305-456-9948
www.mckitchenmiami.com
CUISINE: Italian
DRINKS: Full Bar
SERVING: Lunch-Dinner
PRICE RANGE: $$$
NEIGHBORHOOD: Design District
Another fine dining experience in the Design District, just a couple of blocks from pioneering Michael Schwartz's Michael's Genuine. Here it's Dena Marino, serving up some of the most prized Italian cuisine in Miami. Spinach lasagna, lovely burrata stuffed with roasted squash, charred octopus drenched in olive oil, spaghetti with shrimp—all are excellent. At lunch one day I had a bloody Mary that the waiter told me had ketchup in it. It sounded so terrible. But after tasting it, I ordered 2 more in rapid succession. (Service can be glacial, so tell them if you want things speeded up.)

MICHAEL'S GENUINE FOOD & DRINK

MICHAEL'S GENUINE FOOD & DRINK
130 NE 40th St., Miami
305- 573-5550 / Design District
www.michaelsgenuine.com
CUISINE: American
DRINKS: Full bar
SERVING: Lunch / Dinner
Simple décor, but you didn't come to this world-renowned eatery for the décor. Chef Michael Schwartz (who rose to some prominence on South Beach at the now closed Nemo's) became an international culinary star when he jumped over to the still-dormant Design District and opened this place focusing on locally sourced ingredients. Menu changes as he sees fit, but you can't go wrong with anything you get here. I even get the chicken here. Plain, simple chicken, which I rarely eat in restaurants because it's usually so incredibly awful. Here, though, it's moist and juicy. Indoor-outdoor. Hard to get in during peak times, even in summer! I always sneak in early, whether for lunch (I prefer the bar where I munch on radishes they keep in bowls) or dinner (outside; or inside, a booth is prized). Great staff. Well-balanced wine list. $$$

MORGANS
28 NE 29th St., Miami
305-573-9678 / Wynwood
themorgansrestaurant.com
CUISINE: American
DRINKS: Full bar
SERVING: B'fast / Lunch / Dinner
They took an old Miami house built in the '30s and turned it into a restaurant.

Food's always innovative and trendy. Weekend brunch.

NI.DO CAFFÈ
7295 Biscayne Blvd., Miami
305-960-7022 / Biscayne Corridor
www.nidocaffe.com
CUISINE: Italian
DRINKS: Beer/ Wine
SERVING: Lunch / Dinner
Mozzarella bar. They make it here. Artichoke soufflé, tuna tartare. Very comfy feeling here.

SALUMERIA104
3451 NE First Ave, Miami
305-424-9588 / Midtown
www.salumeria104.com
CUISINE: Italian
DRINKS: Beer & Wine Only
SERVING: Brunch, Lunch & Dinner
PRICE RANGE: $$
Great place for an authentic Italian meal. Menu features a variety of Italian cured meats, pastas, and specials. Menu picks include: Beef lasagna and Antipasto. Nice approachable wine list.

SOYKA
5556 NE 4th Ct., Miami
305-759-3117 / Biscayne Corridor
www.soykarestaurant.com
CUISINE: American Contemporary
DRINKS: Full Bar
SERVING: Lunch / Dinner
Mark Soyka, who made his name on South Beach at the News Café and the Van Dyke on Lincoln Road, was a pioneer when he came to this desolate stretch of Biscayne Boulevard and opened this popular eatery in an old industrial style building. They've lost a lot of business to the new hip spots in Midtown and the Design District, but this is a reliable standby. You'll love it. $$$

SHOKUDO BY WORLD RESOURCE CAFE
4740 NE 2nd Ave., Miami
305-758-7782 / Design District
www.shokudomiami.com
CUISINE: Asian Fusion
DRINKS: Beer & Wine SERVING: Lunch, Dinner
Elegant but casual setting serving tasty dishes like Ahi Tuna Poke, SISIG - Sizzling Pork Cheek Buns and house-made dumplings. Impeccable service. $$

SUGARCANE RAW BAR GRILL
3252 NE 1st Ave., Miami
786 369-0353 / Midtown
http://www.sugarcanerawbargrill.com
CUISINE: International
DRINKS: Full Bar
SERVING: Lunch/ Dinner
One of the hippest spots in Midtown. All kinds of things going on with this menu, which ranges all over the world. Great raw bar items. I find it very expensive. As if by offering "small plates," they can charge you a lot of money for a small portion. Still, the food is incredibly good with creative twists and an unusual use of exotic ingredients that will keep your head spinning. How about bacon-wrapped dates? Sounds awful, right? It's not. A big fat date is stuffed with Manchego cheese, linguiça sausage and then wrapped in bacon. Way busy on weekends. Indoor-outdoor. $$$$

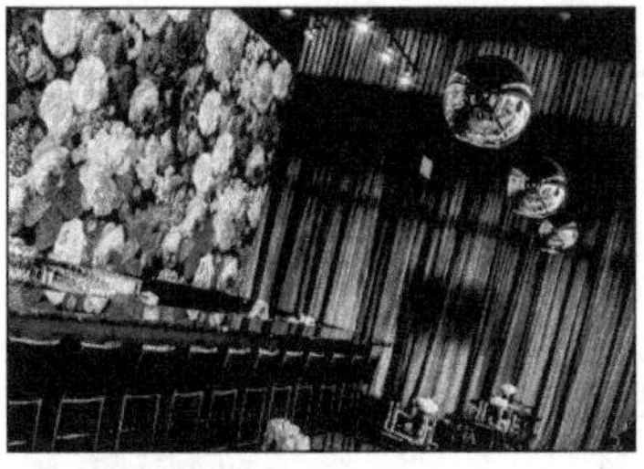

THEA'S MIAMI
1951 NW 7th Ave., Miami
305-777-3777
www.theamiami.com/
CUISINE: Pizza, salads
DRINKS: Beer & Wine Only
SERVING: Breakfast, lunch
PRICE RANGE: $$
NEIGHBORHOOD: Wynwood / Overtown
Not in the best neighborhood, but things are changing rapidly as big investors move into the area. Thea used to be married to Joey Goldman (of Joey's Café in Wynwood—legendary South Beach and Wynwood investor Tony Goldman was Joey's dad). None of this will matter to you, the visitor. What matters is this wonderful little find. Get the pizza with artichoke hearts and arugula. Or go for one of the excellent pasta dishes like rigatoni with ricotta cheese and sausage. Charcuterie and cheese boards, as well as a luscious skirt steak over a bed of arugula, watercress and caramelized shallots.

WYNWOOD KITCHEN & BAR
2550 NW 2nd Ave., Miami
305-772-8959 / Wynwood
www.wynwoodkitchenandbar.com
CUISINE: American
DRINKS: Beer/ Wine
SERVING: Lunch/ Dinner
Tony Goldman was one of the original New York developers who came to South Beach and saw in the Art Deco District what none of the local developers saw: a gold mine. (When he died in 2012, he still owned the Park Central Hotel, his flagship property on Ocean Drive.) He never rested on his laurels. He was a big mover and shaker in Wynwood, owning lots of

property. What Craig Robins wrought in the Design District, Tony Goldman has wrought in Wynwood, to wit: put it on the map. This was his restaurant, and you'll love it. (Son Joey owns the eponymous Italian eatery a few feet away.) The way they've decorated the walls with graffiti-style art will remind you why you're not a decorator: who would have thought of this? Food? Very much a bistro style menu, but with influences all over the place. I like the "clay pots," whole meals served in little pots. Choose from chicken curry, the snapper and mussel curry or the braised beef (my favorite of the three: short ribs, sweet soy, caramelized leeks, pickled chilies - $25). Also a standout: the cod fish oreganata and the hanger steak frites. Satisfying sandwiches and salads as well. Don't forget to walk around the grounds outside to have a look at the graffiti art. $$$

WYNWOOD YARD
56 NW 29th St, Miami
305-351-0366
www.thewynwoodyard.com
CUISINE: Bars, Food Trucks,
DRINKS: Full Bar
SERVING: Lunch & Dinner
PRICE RANGE: $$
NEIGHBORHOOD: Wynwood
Wynwood Yard is a unique spot in Miami's art neighborhood featuring a selection of food trucks, creative eateries and live music at night. It's really quite the scene, and if you're in Wynwood Arts District to check out some of dozens of art galleries in the area, this ought to be one of your stops when you get hungry. Very cool spot. Vendors include: Della Test Kitchen, Kuenko, The Bar at The Yard, World Famous House of Mac, Yoko Matcha, Brazilian Fire, Charcoal Garden Bar + Grill, Wyn-Box, Food Dude, Morgan's Pizza Truck, Doggystyle Miami Hot Dogs, and Pasilla Tacos. Check out websites of each vendor for hours.

DOWNTOWN/ BRICKELL

There really is a lot going on Downtown. From the wizardry of Daniel Boulud at db Bistro Moderne, you'll find everything from high quality Indonesian food for $5 at Bali Café (no credit cards, cash only) to slices of sashimi at Zuma that will cost you twice that for one slice. But it takes some getting used to navigating your way around Downtown. It's congested, everything jammed together, annoying one-way streets, aggravating—and all very exciting. Best is to take someone who knows the area if you're rushed for time.

AREA 31
270 Biscayne Boulevard Way, Miami:
305-424-5234
www.area31restaurant.com
CUISINE: Seafood, Mediterranean
DRINKS: Full Bar
SERVING: B'fast / Lunch / Dinner
Hard to beat the environment they've created down here. From the vantage point of the 16th floor here at the Epic, you get a spectacular view of all the buildings downtown (from inside or outside on their terrace). You feel like you're in a

AREA 31

huge metropolis, surrounded by all these glamorous towers. This is NOT the Miami that you get down on street level.

Anyway, the food and drinks are just as spectacular as the view. (Bring your expense account privileges.) The "Area 31" in the name refers to what I presume some official body has determined is a sustainable fishing area that extends from the Carolinas down along the Florida coast, though this can't possibly be true. Still, it's a great marketing hook and you feel free to order anything you want.

Specialties are seafood prepared with a Mediterranean twist.

Lunch: try the pork belly sliders or the smoked turkey club.

Dinner: focus on the fish: yellowtail snapper, the shrimp ravioli are excellent.

What the chef does quite well is use unusual ingredients in all his dishes. His croquettas have tomato jam, diced plantains and cilantro along with the chorizo. His yellowfin tuna will come with radishes, pickled cucumber, quinoa and shoyu.

Here, you're in the hands of a master. (One of those hands will be in your wallet!) $$$$

ATRIO
Conrad Miami
1395 Brickell Ave., Miami
305-503-6500
http://www.conradmiami.com
CUISINE: American
DRINKS: Full Bar
SERVING: B'fast/Lunch / Dinner
This place is no slouch in the view

AZUL

department, located as it is in a 36-story tower offering stunning views of Biscayne Bay and Miami Beach in the distance.

This is the kind of place that's really good anytime. At breakfast you get a sense of excitement for the day ahead as you look at the view. For lunch, this is as perfect place for a "power lunch," situated as it is in the middle of Downtown, with all the banks and lawyers around you. Dinner get more romantic, again, that damned view.

Softshell crab comes with avocado roll, pear and slaw ($16). Deep fried flounder is yummy with a spicy mango remoulade ($28). Seared striped bass with orange confit and fennel puree (38). And don't overlook the pan roasted kurobuta pork chop with polenta, apple and sweet chili marmalade and green tomato slaw. $34 for a pork chop is pushing it (and pushing it pretty hard, if I say so myself), but hey, you didn't come here to bitch about the prices. 200 wines on their list.

AZUL
Mandarin Oriental
500 Brickell Key Dr., Miami
305-913-8358
www.mandarinoriental.com/miami/fine-dining/azul/
CUISINE: Asian Fusion
DRINKS: Full Bar
SERVING: Dinner
PRICE RANGE: $$$$$

You get a close-up view of Biscayne Bay through floor-to-ceiling windows at night (since they're only open for dinner). One of the most romantic spots in Miami. Wildly creative (and wildly expensive) dishes will knock you off your culinary feet. Things like smoked octopus with cauliflower puree, brown butter babaganoush, eggplant, a "middle plate" portion of 12-hour suckling pig with tempura duck egg, speck air, black truffle pomme puree, pork jus. Or a squab breast with beets, spaetzle and apple butter. Or try the Kobe short ribs. But it comes with white asparagus, black truffles, smoked potato espuma, elderflower watercress coulis and oxen Bordelaise. (You know, it might be interesting to ask them what it would cost if you got all the things that come with the Kobe short ribs, and just didn't get the short ribs.) One visit here will convince you that they are dead serious about the quality and painstaking preparations that go into each and every dish.

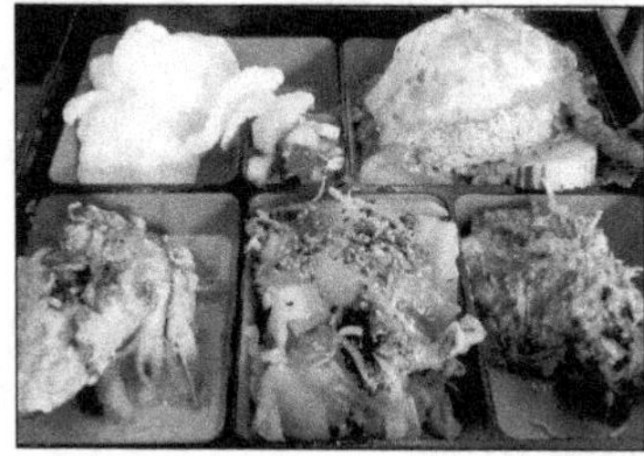

BALI CAFÉ
109 NE 2nd Ave., Miami
305-358-5751
No web site
CUISINE: Indonesia; sushi; Asian fusion
DRINKS: Beer/Wine
SERVING: Lunch / Dinner – CASH ONLY
This place is noted because it was written up in the Herald that low-wage Indonesian cruise ship workers who get like half a day off when their ships come into pick up new passengers head out in droves to this tiny place in Downtown. Well, everybody else started coming here too. And since the underpaid cruise ship workers are only here once a week, you get the rest of the week to try it out. If you've never had this kind of food, get the rijsttafel, which is a kind of sampler. All good food. Cheap. $$. CASH ONLY.

THE BAR AT LEVEL 25
(CONRAD HOTEL)
1395 Brickell Ave., Miami
305-503-6500
www.conradmiami.com
CUISINE: Tapas
DRINKS: Full Bar
SERVING: Lunch / Dinner
PRICE RANGE: $$$$
They serve sandwiches at lunch and have a raw bar with creative tapas dishes in the evening. Another great view of Downtown.

BARU URBANO
901 S. Miami Ave., Miami
305 381-5901
www.barurbano.com
CUISINE: Latin American
DRINKS: Full Bar
SERVING: Lunch / Dinner
PRICE RANGE: $$$
Happening spot that's good for people-watching, especially at the outdoor bar if the weather's right. Their happy hour runs from noon to 8. Wow! Their steak sandwich is called Pepito, and it's really good. Also recommended are the tequenos with dipping sauces. Lunch specials are

$10. Gets packed on the weekends, with a doorman and velvet ropes and the like. Service reminds me of so many places on South Beach: indifferent. Excellent on occasion, sullen at worse.

BOULUD SUD MIAMI
JW Marriott Marquis, 255 Biscayne Blvd. Way, Miami: 305-421-8800
https://www.bouludsud.com/miami/
CUISINE: French, American
DRINKS: Full Bar
SERVING: Lunch / Dinner
PRICE RANGE: $$$$-$$$$
Daniel Boulud's take on American food using Florida ingredients, with his French twist, of course. The result: spectacular. His burger has gotten famous: a stack that includes foie gras, short ribs and black truffles. (Oh, and there's a burger stuffed in there too.) Bring a Lipitor. (Honestly, avoid the burger and focus on the fish.)

CAPITAL GRILLE
444 Brickell Ave., Miami
305 374-4500
http://www.thecapitalgrille.com
CUISINE: Steakhouse
DRINKS: Full Bar
SERVING: Lunch weekdays/Dinner nightly
PRICE RANGE: $$$$
Dry-aged steaks and an award-winning wine list are the draw at this "power lunch" spot. Same sort of menu you already know about. Still, the lobster mac & cheese is a standout.

CIPRIANI
465 Brickell Ave., Miami
786-329-4090
www.cipriani.com
CUISINE: Italian
DRINKS: Full Bar
SERVING: Lunch-Dinner daily
PRICE RANGE: $$$$
NEIGHBORHOOD: Brickell
The Cipriani family has made good use of its legendary history, parlaying it into a chain of upmarket restaurants around the world. But they've come a long way since Ernest Hemingway drank in the modest Harry's Bar in Venice. A long way indeed. Ignazio Cipriani is great grandson to Giuseppe, who opened Harry's in 1931. There are 2 levels to this location, and they seat a whopping 400, so it's a massive undertaking. Floor-to-ceiling windows look out onto panoramic views of the Bay. White leather seats and walnut paneling add to the look. The service is professional, but the two times I've been, the waiters were bossy to the point of rudeness. There's way too much steering you to this dish or that wine. Italian

specialties are good, but plan on a LONG lunch or dinner. They're in no rush and you better not be.

CRAZY ABOUT YOU
1155 Brickell Bay Dr. #101, Miami:
305-377-4442
www.crazyaboutyourestaurant.com
CUISINE: Mediterranean, Italian, Spanish
DRINKS: Full Bar
SERVING: Lunch / Dinner
Great views. Widely varied menu: chihuahua cheese appetizer; lentil soup, spinach salad; half roasted chicken; red pepper hummus; slow braised steak with creamy arborio rice.

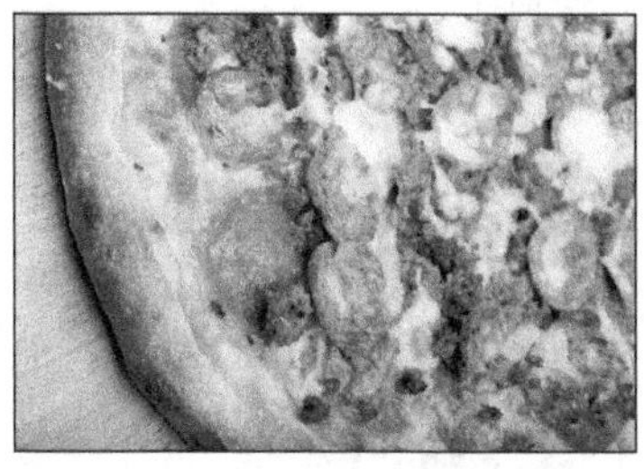

CRUST
668 NW 5TH St., Miami
305-371-7065
www.crust-usa.com
CUISINE: Pizza / Mediterranean
DRINKS: Beer & Wine Only
SERVING: Dinner; closed Mondays
PRICE RANGE: $$
Chef Klime Kovaceski's Italian eatery specializes in pizza with gourmet toppings like figs, pesto-artichoke and fresh basil. The creative menu offers a variety of Mediterranean dishes from chef Kovaceski's personal recipes. Delivery available.

CEVICHE 105
105 NE 3rd Ave., Miami
305-577-3454
www.ceviche105.com
CUISINE: Peruvian
DRINKS: Full Bar
SERVING: Lunch / Dinner
Try the "Sudado Mixto" ($14.95), poached fish and seafood stew with potatoes, onions and red pepper slices. $$

DOLORES, BUT YOU CAN CALL ME LOLITA
1000 S. Miami Ave., Miami
305-403-3103
www.doloreslolita.com
CUISINE: American
DRINKS: Full Bar
SERVING: Lunch / Dinner
Romantic setting (except when it's jammed on weekend nights). Try to get a table on the patio upstairs. Pappardelle with kobe beef Bolognese; filet mignon funghi. $$$

EDGE STEAK & BAR
Four Seasons Hotel, 1435 Brickell Ave, Miami, 305-381-3190
www.edgerestaurantmiami.com
CUISINE: Seafood/Steakhouse/American (New)
DRINKS: Full bar
SERVING: Dinner
PRICE RANGE: $$$
NEIGHBORHOOD: Brickell
Luxury steakhouse located in the Four Season Hotel so expect the best. Located on the 7th floor of the Four Season, this eatery offers a great dining experience. Menu picks include: Pork & Pistachio Terrine and Chicken Liver and Foie Gras Pâté. Great choice for brunch.

FOOQ'S
1035 N Miami Ave, Miami
786-536-2749
www.fooqsmiami.com
CUISINE: Persian / American (New)
DRINKS: Beer & Wine Only
SERVING: Dinner Tues-Sun; Lunch on Sun; Closed Mon
PRICE RANGE: $$$
NEIGHBORHOOD: Downtown
Located in downtown Miami's "nightclub" district, this unique eatery offers American fare with a Persian twist. Favorites: Braised lamb; Khoresh (which is Persian stew) and Delmonico steak. Reservations recommended.

FRATELLI MILANO
213 SE 1st St., Miami
305-373-2300
www.ristorantefratellimilano.com
CUISINE: Italian
DRINKS: Beer/Wine
SERVING: Lunch / Dinner; closed Sunday
PRICE RANGE: $$-$$$
Bucatini san Babila, thick pasta with sweet Italian sausage, broccoli, garlic, pecorino cheese in a tomato sauce; Fettuccine Allo Scoglio, homemade fettuccine, sauteed shrimp, scallops, calamari and mussels in a white wine sauce; lobster ravioli; Fiocchi di Pera.

GARCIA'S SEAFOOD GRILLE & FISH MARKET
398 NW N. River Dr., Miami
305-375-0765
www.garciasseafoodgrill.com
CUISINE: Seafood
DRINKS: Full Bar
SERVING: Lunch / Dinner
PRICE RANGE: $-$$$
Long a popular seafood eatery on the Miami River. Just concentrate on the seafood, seafood, seafood. During stone crab season, they usually have a 2-4-1

GARCIA'S SEAFOOD GRILLE & FISH MARKET

special on Friday. A friend of mine with a boat goes down almost every Friday during season to get them, tying up at the dock in front of this place. Makes for a great afternoon. (I'm not listing Casablanca, which is just next door, but, many people prefer it over Garcia's. Me? I can't really tell the difference. They're both excellent.)

GRAZIANO'S RESTAURANT BRICKELL
177 SW 7th St., Miami
305 860-1426
http://www.grazianosgroup.com

CUISINE: Argentine
DRINKS: full bar
SERVING: B'fast / Lunch / Dinner
PRICE RANGE: $$$
Argentine steak house. Top quality meats, as would be expected. There's a great bakery here, so you have to go through it to the restaurant behind. Pastas with chicken is good if you're not into meats. There are chips with truffle oil dribbled over them. Also the spinach gnocchi. They have an excellent selection of Malbecs here – ask them to suggest a reasonably priced one (don't let them give you one for more than $35) if you're not familiar with this rich, red Argentine wine.

HARD ROCK CAFE
Bayside Marketplace
401 Biscayne Blvd., Miami
305 377-3110
http://www.hardrock.com
CUISINE: American
DRINKS: Full Bar
SERVING: Lunch / Dinner
PRICE RANGE: $$$
You know what to expect here. Nothing too different. Standard chain menu. Nice overlooking marina at Bayside. Indoor-outdoor.

Il GABBIANO
335 S. Biscayne Blvd., Miami
305-373-0063
www.ilgabbianomia.com
CUISINE: Italian
DRINKS: Full Bar
SERVING: Lunch weekdays, noon to 3; dinner from 5; closed Sunday.
Where the Miami River meets the Bay, you'll find this super excellent Italian restaurant. Everything you've heard about it is true: it may be the best Italian restaurant in all of Florida, one of the best in the country. (Scarpetta in the Fontainebleau is right up there with this.) Fried zucchini, gnocchi with gorgonzola, mushroom ravioli, grilled calamari is excellent; alla Scarpariello; spaghetti alla carbonara; ricotta cheesecake. Whatever pennies you have, this place is worth the last one. $$$$$

KAORI BY WALTER MARTINO
1250 S Miami Ave, Miami
786-805-6006
www.kaoribywm.com/
CUISINE: Japanese/Italian/Asian Fusion
DRINKS: Full bar
SERVING: Dinner; closed Monday
PRICE RANGE: $$$$
NEIGHBORHOOD: Brickell
Modern 24-seat eatery with high-tech futuristic décor including wall projections that change frequently. The food is appealing visually and delicious. Favorites include: Bresola Wagyu Beef Roll and Black Sea bass Sushiotto. Unusual menu options include edible gold and silver with matching price tags. Definitely a place for high rollers and the chef has been dubbed "Million Dollar Chef".

KIKI ON THE RIVER
450 NW North River Dr, Miami

786-502-3243
www.kikiontheriver.com
CUISINE: Greek/Mediterranean
DRINKS: Beer & Wine Only
SERVING: Full Bar
PRICE RANGE: $$$$
NEIGHBORHOOD: Downtown
Chic waterfront eatery on the Miami River offers a menu of traditional Greek cuisine and seafood. It's a big spot that they spent a fortune on, with wooden planks outside facing the river, where you can dock a boat if you have one. It's hot in the summer, even with the fans whirring all around you. There is an indoor dining room, but it's no fun compared to outside. Favorites: Grilled octopus and Grilled scallops. Great cocktails. Can get crowded on the weekends and when they turn up the music, it's hard to bear. (Tip: save a fortune by coming during the week for lunch when they have a very reasonably priced prix fixe.)

KOMODO

801 Brickell Ave, Miami
305-534-2211
www.komodomiami.com
CUISINE: Chinese/Asian Fusion
DRINKS: Full bar
SERVING: Lunch/Dinner; Dinner only on Sat & Sun
PRICE RANGE: $$$$
NEIGHBORHOOD: Brickell
Upscale eatery offering a high-end menu of Southeastern Asian fare. Massive multi-level dining room with dining indoors and out. Family-style menu items include favorites like: Lobster Dynamite and Grilled Szechuan Beef.

LA LOGGIA RISTORANTE AND LOUNGE

68 W. Flagler St., Miami
305-373-4800
www.laloggiamiami.com
CUISINE: Italian
DRINKS: Full Bar
SERVING: Lunch / Dinner
Inexpensive, family style Italian food. $$$

LA MOON

97 SW 8th St., Miami
305-860-6209
No Website
CUISINE: Colombian
DRINKS: Beer/Wine
SERVING: Lunch / Dinner/Late night
PRICE RANGE: $
Excellent quality cheap Colombian food.

LARGO BAR & GRILL
Bayside, 401 Biscayne Blvd., Miami
305-374-9706
www.largobarandgrill.com
CUISINE: American
DRINKS: Full Bar
SERVING: Lunch / Dinner
Avoid Hooters and the Hard Rock and opt for this if you're in the downtown "tourist trap" called Bayside. Buffalo chicken salad, Philly cheesesteak, Angus sliders, crab cake sandwich, seafood Alfredo, chicken parm, scampi over pasta. $$-$$$

LOS GAUCHITOS STEAKHOUSE
The Doubletree Grand
1717 N. Bayshore Dr., Miami
305-377-3133
www.biscaynebay.doubletree.com
CUISINE: Argentine steakhouse
DRINKS: Full Bar
SERVING: Lunch / Dinner
It's OK, but if this is the kind of food you want, there are many other better places similarly priced. Keep reading. $$$

MORTON'S
THE STEAKHOUSE MIAMI
1200 Brickell Ave., Miami
305-400-9990
http://www.mortons.com/miami
CUISINE: Steakhouse
DRINKS: Full Bar
SERVING: L (weekdays)/D
You know all about it. $$$$

NAOE
661Brickell Key Dr, Miami
305-947-6263
www.naoemiami.com
CUISINE: Seafood/Steakhouse /Live Raw Food
DRINKS: Beer & Wine Only
SERVING: Dinner
PRICE RANGE: $$$$
NEIGHBORHOOD: Brickell
Contemporary Japanese bistro offering a creative fixed-price (Omakase) menu. Note there's no sign on the front door so you must look for the number 661. Definitely a culinary experience for fans of sushi and the chef offers seconds of any piece of sushi served during your meal. Not for the budget diners.

NOVECENTO
1414 Brickell Ave., Miami
305-403-0900
www.novecento.com
CUISINE: Contemporary Argentine
DRINKS: Full Bar
SERVING: Lunch / Dinner
Not just steaks; excellent seafood as well. $$-$$$

PEGA GRILL
15 E. Flagler St., Miami
305-808-6666
www.pegagrill.com
CUISINE: Greek
DRINKS: Beer/Wine
SERVING: Lunch
Nice spot for good Greek food that's fast and cheap. $$

PERRICONE'S
15 SE 10th St., Miami
305-374-9449
www.perricones.com
CUISINE: Italian
DRINKS: Full Bar
SERVING: Lunch / Dinner
A home-style Italian eatery that's situated

in a 200-year-old house brought down from Vermont. It's part market, bakery, bar and restaurant. Food's great, atmosphere genuinely charming. $$

PIZZARIUM
69 E. Flagler St., Miami
305-381-6025
www.pizzariummiami.com
CUISINE: Pizza
DRINKS: Beer & Wine
SERVING: Lunch, Dinner
New York feel but definitely Roman style pizza made famous in Miami. They serve 27 different kinds of pizza. Great prices for 5-star pizza. $

RIVER OYSTER BAR
also known as
RIVER SEAFOOD & OYSTER BAR

650 S. Miami Ave., Miami
305-530-1915
www.therivermiami.com
CUISINE: Seafood
DRINKS: Full Bar
SERVING: Lunch / Dinner
PRICE RANGE: $$$
Though they have a substantial menu, I don't think I've sat at a table here in years. I always slither up to the bar and order a couple of dozen oysters mixed from the selection they currently have available. And have a bottle of wine or a couple of beers.

RIVERWALK CAFE

Hyatt Regency Miami
400 SE 2nd Ave., Miami
305 358-1234
www.hyatt.com/en-US/hotel/florida/hyatt-regency-miami/miarm/dining
CUISINE: American; some Latin
DRINKS: Full Bar
SERVING: B'fast / Lunch / Dinner
PRICE RANGE: $$$
Typical hotel restaurant offering the expected American menu with a few "Latin" items thrown in to remind you that you're in Miami. Better than eating here, go outside and get the real thing.

ROSA MEXICANO

900 S. Miami Ave., Miami
786-425-1001
www.rosamexicano.com
CUISINE: Mexican
DRINKS: Full Bar
SERVING: Lunch / Dinner
PRICE RANGE: $$$
There's a Rosa outpost on Lincoln Road, but it seems so much more expensive than this one Downtown. But the food's the real thing.

SOYA & POMODORO

120 NE 1st St., Miami: 305-381-9511
www.soyaepomodoro.com
CUISINE: Italian
DRINKS: Beer/Wine
SERVING: Lunch (weekdays); Dinner (Thursday-Saturday)
PRICE RANGE: $-$$
This charming little spot is located in the old Dupont Building, so you're immediately enclosed in an architectural style that will make you feel like you're in Europe. Food is good, cheap Italian, from the south.

SPARKY'S ROADSIDE RESTAURANT & BAR
204 NE 1st St., Miami: 305-377-2877
www.sparkysroadsidebarbecue.com
CUISINE: Barbeque
DRINKS: Beer/Wine
SERVING: Lunch / Dinner
BBQ in the dry-rubbed style. Very nice. They make their own sauces. $-$$

SUVICHE
49 SW 11th St., Miami
305-960-7097
www.suviche.com
CUISINE: Sushi, Peruvian, Japanese
DRINKS: Beer/Wine
SERVING: Lunch / Dinner
Tiny, tiny place serving excellent Peruvian-Japanese food. $$

TABLE 40
Intercontinental, 100 Chopin Plaza, Miami: 305-372-4710
www.icmiamihotel.com
CUISINE: American
DRINKS: full bar
SERVING: dinner
Elegant décor highlights the ambience here in this fine restaurant. Start with the corn gazpacho; smoked braised short ribs; lobster salad. $$$$

TORO TORO
Intercontinental
100 Chopin Plaza, Miami
305-372-4710
www.torotoromiami.com
CUISINE: Latin American, Steakhouse, Tapas
DRINKS: Full Bar
SERVING: Lunch, Dinner
Authentic Latin American dishes in Miami's iconic InterContinental Hotel. Delicious menu items include dozens of tapas, flat bread pizza, and lamb anticuchos. Also grouper pan-roasted and a caldo de pollo. For lunch, get the pepito steak sandwich. $$$

TRAPICHE ROOM
JW Marriott Hotel
1109 Brickell Ave., Miami
305 329-3500
http://www.marriott.com/miajw
CUISINE: American
DRINKS: Full Bar
SERVING:Lunch / Dinner
Quite nice to find such a fine dining experience within the Marriott, especially with the Marriott Marquis just a few feet away boasting Daniel Boulud's press-snatching db Bistro Moderne. Here you'll find Mediterranean cuisine meticulously prepared and attentively served in a pleasantly romantic setting. Leek soup, seafood crepe, chocolate mousse. $$$$

TRULUCK'S SEAFOOD, STEAK & CRABHOUSE
777 Brickell Ave., Miami
305-579-0035
www.trulucks.com
CUISINE: Seafood, Steakhouse
DRINKS: Full Bar
SERVING: Lunch (weekdays) /Dinner nightly
PRICE RANGE: $$$-$$$$
Most steakhouses offer big lobsters just because they can, but their hearts are with the steaks. Here, it's just the opposite. While you can get really great steaks, their hearts are with the seafood. (They catch their own stone crabs, and it's cheaper than Joe's). Fine menu complemented by very good service.

WOLFGANG'S STEAKHOUSE
315 S Biscayne Blvd., Miami
305-487-7130
www.wolfgangssteakhouse.net/miami
CUISINE: American; steakhouse
DRINKS: Full Bar
SERVING: Lunch-Dinner
PRICE RANGE: $$$$
NEIGHBORHOOD: Brickell
How many steakhouses can Miami absorb? If we had to have another one, at least we got a good one with Wolfgang's. The Porterhouse for 2 is a marvel of texture and flavor. They have lobster and sea bass on the menu, but stick to the steaks. Wolfgang Zwiener was head waiter at the legendary Peter Luger's in Brooklyn before leaving to open his flagship location on Park Avenue. Miami is a better place because he came here, too. In fact, I think it's way better than Peter Luger. Oh, and here you can use a credit card, useless at Luger's, which even after all these years, still only take Cash.

ZEST
200 S Biscayne Blvd, Miami
305-374-9873
www.zestmiami.com
CUISINE: American (New)/Caribbean
DRINKS: Full bar
SERVING: Lunch & Dinner; Dinner only on Sat; closed Sun
PRICE RANGE: $$
NEIGHBORHOOD: Downtown
Modern eatery with a menu of creative island fare from Chef Cindy Hutson. Menu favorites include: Ceviche, Yellowtail snapper, and Cornish hen. Regulars rave about the salmon coated with coffee and cocoa. Save room for the amazing bread pudding.

ZUMA
Epic Hotel
270 Biscayne Blvd. Way, Miami
305 577-0277
http://www.zumarestaurant.com
CUISINE: Japanese
DRINKS: Full Bar
SERVING: Lunch (till 3); dinner from 6.
PRICE RANGE: $$$$
This rave-inducing spot will thrill you if you're into Japanese fine food. Lobster tempura, ribeye with wafu sauce, salmon teriyaki, grilled scallops, black cod, mushroom risotto. You'll love the view overlooking the docks and the River.

LITTLE HAVAVA

While there's a lot more to Little Havana than Cuban food, it's the Cuban food you come for.

ANTIGUA GUATEMALA CAFETERIA
2741 W Flagler St., Miami
305-643-0304
No web site
CUISINE: Central American
DRINKS: Beer/ Wine
SERVING: B'fast / Lunch / Dinner
Although the name suggests differently, this eatery serves up mostly Central American dishes. Pupusas (corn tortillas stuffed with cheese, beans, chicharron, or a revuelto, a combination of all three), a variety of daily soups, stuffed peppers, pickled pork and churrasco. $

CASA JUANCHO

2436 SW 8th St., Miami
305-642-2524
http://www.casajuancho.com
CUISINE: Spanish
DRINKS: Full Bar
SERVING: Lunch / Dinner
PRICE RANGE: $$$$
In this well-known eatery, Spanish delicacies include baby eel and hand carved ham from acorn fed Iberian pigs.

DON CAMARON SEAFOOD GRILL

501 NW 37 Ave., Miami
305-642-6767
www.doncamaronrestaurant.com
CUISINE: Seafood
DRINKS: Beer/ Wine
SERVING: B'fast / Lunch / Dinner
PRICE RANGE: $-$$
Here you will find everything seafood; fish dishes come with rice and your choice of plantains or French fries. Get there early; this place fills up fast.

EL JACALITO TAQUERIA MEXICANA

3622 W Flagler St., Miami
305-443-1336
www.jacalitomexicanrestaurant.com
CUISINE: Mexican
DRINKS: Beer/ Wine
SERVING: B'fast / Lunch / Dinner
You will feel right at home in this small and quaint restaurant. Although they serve up traditional Mexican dishes, it's the tacos that are a must have. Huge selection of tacos including tongue, cow cheek, cochinita pibil (shredded pork), chorizo, beef, chicken, and vegetables. $-$$

EL PALACIO DE LOS JUGOS

5721 W Flagler St., Miami
305-264-1503
www.elpalaciodelosjugos.com
CUISINE: Cuban
DRINKS: No Alcohol
SERVING: B'fast / Lunch / Dinner
This landmark is a one-stop shop including a market overflowing with fresh fruits and vegetables and a juice bar serving an array of juices and batidos. $

LA CAMARONERA FISH MARKET
1952 W. Flagler St., Miami
305-642-3322
http://garciabrothersseafood.com
CUISINE: Cuban Seafood
DRINKS: No Alcohol
SERVING: B'fast / Lunch / Dinner
No seats in this eatery, just a counter that you can lean on making this place a true Cuban fish-fry. Get there early, it fills up fast. $

LA CARRETA
3632 SW 8th St., Miami
305-444-7501
www.lacarreta.com
CUISINE: Cuban
DRINKS: Full Bar
SERVING: B'fast / Lunch / Dinner
Although not the most gourmet of Cuban cuisine, it is a great place to get traditional dishes. Great daily specials. $$

LA CASITA CUBAN CUISINE
3805 SW 8th St., Miami
305-448-8224
www.lasvegascubancuisine.com
CUISINE: Cuban
DRINKS: Full Bar
SERVING: Lunch / Dinner
Surprisingly low-key and mellow, this place serves up delicious typical Cuban dishes at affordable prices. $

LAS TAPAS DE ROSA
449 SW 8th St., Miami: 305-856-9788
www.tapasderosa.com
CUISINE: Spanish, Tapas
DRINKS: Beer & Wine
SERVING: Lunch, Dinner
This little family-run restaurant is known for serving some of the best tapas in Miami, almost all under $10. Old World feel, friendly service, and extensive Spanish wine list. $$

VERSAILLES
3555 SW 8th St., Miami
305-444-0240
www.versaillesrestaurant.com
CUISINE: Cuban
DRINKS: Full Bar
SERVING: B'fast / Lunch / Dinner
A staple of the Cuban community, this is as authentic as it gets. The Cuban coffee is a must have. $$

CORAL GABLES

Coral Gables has never been known for excitement. In fact, the city fathers are so aware of the city's image that they seek to control just about everything, from the size of a realtor's sign on a lawn to the color of a newspaper box on the corner. But as dull as the Gables can be, one place where the excitement has always been at the uppermost level is in the field of fine dining. Even with the explosion of great restaurants on South Beach (and more lately, Downtown), the swank eateries in the Gables have held their own, and make the "City Beautiful" really a "City Bountiful."

BRASSERIE CENTRAL
320 San Lorenzo Ave, Coral Gables,
786-536-9388
www.brasseriecentralmiami.com
CUISINE: French
DRINKS: Full Bar
SERVING: Dinner
PRICE RANGE: $$
NEIGHBORHOOD: Merrick Park/Coral Gables
Cute brasserie serving classic French fare with the atmosphere of a Parisian café. Menu picks: Saumon Fume Ecossais (smoked Salmon) and fresh Pate. Raw bar. Nice selection of wines and champagne.

BULLA GASTROBAR
2500 Ponce De Leon Blvd,
Coral Gables, 786-509-7751
www.bullamiami.com
CUISINE: Spanish/Tapas Bar
DRINKS: Full Bar
SERVING: Lunch & Dinner
PRICE RANGE: $$
NEIGHBORHOOD: Coral Gables
Popular eatery serving Spanish and Catalan dishes. Favorites: Patatas Bravas and Huevos Bulla. Variety of tapas (more than 20) and daily specials.

CAFFE ABBRACCI
318 Aragon Ave., Coral Gables
305-441-0700
http://www.caffeabbracci.com
CUSINE: Italian
DRINKS: Full Bar
SERVING: Lunch / Dinner
True to his native Venezia, owner Nino Pernetti continues his time-honored tradition of bringing quintessential classic Northern Italian dishes to his customers in this "power" lunch and dinner spot. A lot of big shots eat here, but Nino makes them pay for the privilege. Indoor-outdoor. $$$$

CANTON AND SUSHI MAKI
2614 Ponce de Leon Blvd.,
Coral Gables: 305-448-3736
http://www.cantonrestaurants.com
CUSINE: Sushi
DRINKS: Beer/Wine
SERVING: Lunch / Dinner
Good Chinese and sushi since 1975, specializing in generously portioned Chinese cuisine served family style for dine-in, take-out, delivery and catering. $$

CHRISTY'S
3101 Ponce de Leon Blvd.,
Coral Gables: 305-446-1400
http://www.christysrestaurant.com
CUSINE: Steakhouse
DRINKS: Full Bar
SERVING: Dinner
Diners at this Miami landmark restaurant enjoy the famous Caesar salad, aged Midwestern beef and the daily fresh Florida seafood. Impossible to go wrong here. $$$$

EATING HOUSE
804 Ponce De Leon Blvd, Coral Gables
305-448-6524
www.eatinghousemiami.com
CUISINE: American (New)
DRINKS: Beer & Wine
SERVING: Lunch & Dinner, Lunch only on Sat; closed Mondays
PRICE RANGE: $$
NEIGHBORHOOD:
Small eatery serving a menu of locally sourced dishes. Menu picks: Pasta carbonara and Chicken & waffles. Usually busy with a wait. Reservations recommended.

FONTANA
The Biltmore
1200 Anastasia Ave., Coral Gables:
305-913-3200
http://www.biltmorehotel.com
CUSINE: Mediterranean
DRINKS: Full Bar
SERVING: B'fast / Lunch / Dinner
Enjoy authentic Italian cuisine in a casual brasserie featuring outdoor dining in a courtyard setting. Main reason to come here is to see the famous hotel. $$$$

FRATELLINO
264 Miracle Mile, Coral Gables
786-452-0068
No Website
CUISINE: Italian
DRINKS: Beer & Wine Only
SERVING: Lunch/Dinner;
Dinner-only on Sun
PRICE RANGE: $$
NEIGHBORHOOD: Coral Gables
Small intimate eatery offering delicious Italian fare. Menu picks include: Risotto alla Pescatora and Risotto alla Pescatora. Also a big favorite is the fried calamari & zucchini. Delicious tiramisu and cheesecake.

FRENCHIE'S DINER
2618 Galiano St, Coral Gables
305-442-4554
www.frenchiesdiner.com
CUISINE: French
DRINKS: Beer & Wine
SERVING: Lunch & Dinner;
closed Sun & Mon
PRICE RANGE: $$
NEIGHBORHOOD: Coral Gables
Friendly eatery offering typical diner fare along with creative daily specials. Favorites: Duck Club Sandwich and Risotto with wild mushrooms.

GRAZIANO'S
394 Giralda Ave., Coral Gables
305-774 3599
http://www.grazianosgroup.com
CUSINE: Argentine Steakhouse
DRINKS: Full Bar
SERVING: Lunch / Dinner
This restaurant is a traditional Argentinean steakhouse. A nice experience for meat and wine lovers. Also pastas, salads and seafood. $$$

HILLSTONE RESTAURANT
201 Miracle Mile, Coral Gables
305-529-0141
www.hillstone.com
CUISINE: American (New)/Sushi
DRINKS: Full bar
SERVING: Lunch/Dinner
PRICE RANGE: $$$
NEIGHBORHOOD: Coral Gables
Upscale restaurant offering a menu of steak, sushi, seafood, and pastas. Upscale chain eatery featuring steak,

seafood & pasta alongside specialty cocktails. Great meat sandwiches and amazing salads. Try their signature dessert tres leches with fresh fruit. Nice wine selection. Reservations a must on weekends.

LA PALMA RISTORANTE
116 Alhambra Circle, Coral Gables
305 445-8777
http://www.lapalmaristorante.com
CUSINE: Italian
DRINKS: Full Bar
SERVING: Lunch / Dinner
Northern Italian cuisine. Located in a restored historic building. Tree-covered courtyard with its stone fountain is both relaxing and romantic. The inside dining room's fine art gives guests the feeling of dining in a gallery. Outdoor dining. $$$$

LIBERTY CAFFE
997 N. Greenway Drive, Coral Gables: 305-392-1211
http://www.libertycaffe.com
CUSINE: Italian
DRINKS: Beer/Wine
SERVING: B'fast / Lunch / Dinner
This is the ideal neighborhood spot for a morning coffee or a cool gelato on a warm afternoon. House-made gelatos, pressed sandwiches, oven-baked pizza breads, specialty coffees and espresso. $$

MESAMAR
264 Giralda Ave, Coral Gables, 305-640-8448
www.mesamar.com
CUISINE: Seafood
DRINKS: Full bar
SERVING: Lunch & Dinner
PRICE RANGE: $$$$
MesaMar serves delicious seafood fusion with an Oriental influence. Favorites include: Tuna & lobster tacos and Calamari.

MORTON'S THE STEAKHOUSE
2333 Ponce De Leon Blvd.,
Coral Gables: 305 442-1662
http://www.mortons.com/coralgables
CUSINE: Steakhouse
DRINKS: Full Bar
SERVING: Lunch / Dinner
For more than 30 years this restaurant has served the finest quality food, featuring USDA prime-aged beef, fresh

fish and seafood, big salads, delicious appetizers and elegant desserts. Indoor-outdoor. $$$$

ORTANIQUE ON THE MILE
278 Miracle Mile, Coral Gables
305-446-7710
http://www.cindyhutsoncuisine.com
CUSINE: Caribbean
DRINKS: Full Bar
SERVING: Dinner
Fusion of American, Caribbean, Latin and Asian cuisine, served in a colorful tropical ambience. Great for people-watching on the Mile. $$$

PASCAL'S ON PONCE
2611 Ponce De Leon Blvd, Coral Gables, 305-444-2024
http://www.pascalmiami.com
CUISINE: French
DRINKS: Full Bar
SERVING: Lunch & Dinner, Dinner only on Sat; closed on Sundays
PRICE RANGE: $$$$
NEIGHBORHOOD: Coral Gables
Cozy bistro serving modern French fare. Favorites: Scallops and Crab cakes. Nice dessert selection. Impressive wine selection. Upscale dining experience.

RED FISH GRILL
9610 Old Cutler Road, Miami
305- 668-8788
http://www.redfishgrill.net
CUSINE: Seafood
DRINKS: Beer/Wine
SERVING: Dinner
Located on the shore of Biscayne Bay in Matheson Hammock Park, this restaurant is a breath of fresh air at the water's edge. Get the pan-fried snapper ($30). The main treat here is the "old Florida" setting. Indoor-outdoor. $$$

RED KOI THAI & SUSHI LOUNGE
317 Miracle Mile, Coral Gables
305-446-2690
http://www.redkoilounge.com
CUSINE: Sushi/Thai
DRINKS: Full Bar
SERVING: Dinner
Asian fusion. Indoor-outdoor. $$$

RINCON ARGENTINO
2345 SW 37th Ave., Coral Gables
305-444-2494
http://www.rinconargentino.com
CUSINE: Latin/American
DRINKS: Full Bar
SERVING: Lunch / Dinner
Fine meats and homemade pastas in this Argentine eatery. $$$

SAWA
Village of Merrick Park
360 San Lorenzo Ave., Coral Gables
305-447-6555
http://www.sawarestaurant.com
CUSINE: Mediterranean
DRINKS: Full Bar
SERVING: Lunch / Dinner
Mediterranean and Japanese cuisines. (Huh?) Chef Jouvens Jean merges an innovative sushi menu with a memorable ensemble of tapas and entrees. Inside there are white walls, white chandeliers, white leather upholstery, vividly colorful interactive 3D artworks by Chady Elias, and an LED light show behind the bar. On the patio, there are billowing white curtains and white leather sofas, where guests can puff away on flavored Hookahs. (Well…) $$$$

SEASONS 52
321 Miracle Mile, Coral Gables
305-442-8552
http://www.seasons52.com
CUSINE: American
DRINKS: Full Bar
SERVING: Lunch / Dinner
Comfy grill and wine bar always seems to have a youngish, attractive crowd and the bar scene is fun, too. They emphasize fresh ingredients. (The flatbreads here can feed two, and they're cheap, cheap, cheap!) $$-$$$

THE SEVEN DIALS
2030 Douglas Rd, Miami
786-542-1603
www.sevendialsmiami.com
CUISINE: Gastropub/American (New)
DRINKS: Beer & Wine Only
SERVING: Lunch/Dinner; Dinner only on Sat; closed Sun
PRICE RANGE: $$
NEIGHBORHOOD: Coral Gables
Casual eatery offering American comfort

food with a British flair. Intimate dining with a small but unique menu offering delicacies like Bone marrow. Bar menu of local brews and wines.

SHULA'S 347 GRILL
6915 Red Road, Coral Gables
305-665-9661
www.shulas347gables.com
CUSINE: American
DRINKS: Full Bar
SERVING: Lunch / Dinner
This restaurant is named in honor of Hall of Fame football coach Don Shula. It follows a long line of successful restaurants, all founded on the same famous tradition of Shula's Steak Houses. Indoor, outdoor. Lotsa fun, really. $$$$

SPRING CHICKEN
1514 South Dixie Hwy, Coral Gables, 305-504-2704
www.eatspringchicken.com
CUISINE: Southern/Traditional American
DRINKS: Full bar
SERVING: Lunch & Dinner
PRICE RANGE: $$$
NEIGHBORHOOD: Coral Gables
Bright and airy restaurant with simple décor and down home atmosphere. They stand by their motto: Live well. Eat Well. Love every Bite. Here you'll find a menu of classic southern fare like southern fried chicken with biscuits. Like sister eatery Yardbird, the customers leave satisfied.

SWINE SOUTHERN TABLE & BAR
2415 Ponce De Leon Blvd., Coral Gables: 786-360-6433
www.runpigrun.com
CUISINE: Southern, Barbeque
DRINKS: Full Bar
SERVING: Lunch, Dinner & Brunch
PRICE RANGE: $$$
The team behind Yardbird and Khong River on South Beach have opened this Temple to Pork down in the staid Gables. It's a tiny place with not that many seats, and no reservations, so expect a wait on the weekends. (Or better yet, go for lunch. It's not as loud with the obnoxiously "hip" music.) Food is expertly prepared, as I expected it would be, served by a smart young staff that bristles with enthusiasm. The bar specializes in cocktails with a bourbon accent, and they have a huge selection. There's a Caesar salad loaded up with pork shoulder that you'll think is the best version of that tired old staple that you've had in years. The brisket is superior. The burger is a mix of short rib, pork, and brisket that's to die for. Desserts are suitably decadent.

TARPON BEND RAW BAR & GRILL
65 Miracle Mile, Coral Gables
305-444-3210
www.tarponbendrawbarandgrill.com
CUISINE: Seafood
DRINKS: Full bar
SERVING: Lunch/Dinner
PRICE RANGE: $$
NEIGHBORHOOD: Coral Gables
Friendly spot for dining alone or with friends with a nice diverse menu. Favorites include: Beef Short Rib Dinner and Seafood Fettuccini. Every Thursday they have Mojito Madness offering happy hour prices on fresh fruit mojitos with flavors like watermelon, blackberry, grapefruit, pineapple, peach, and raspberry.

THREEFOLD CAFÉ
141 Giralda Ave, Coral Gables
305-704-8007
www.threefoldcafe.com
CUISINE: Australian/Cafe
DRINKS: Full bar
SERVING: Breakfast & Lunch; Dinner on Thur, Fri & Sat
PRICE RANGE: $$
NEIGHBORHOOD: Downtown
Great choice for a gourmet breakfast or brunch serving top notch coffee and creative breakfast treats. Delicious breads, benedicts, and French toast. Fresh juices and homemade breads.

TWO SISTERS RESTAURANT
Hyatt Regency
50 Alhambra Plaza, Coral Gables
305- 441-1234
https://coralgables.regency.hyatt.com/en/hotel/dining/TwoSistersRestaurant.html
CUSINE: French/Greek/Mediterranean
DRINKS: Full Bar
SERVING: B'fast / Lunch / Dinner
With the wide variety of things going on with this menu, they should have named it Four Sisters Who Can't Make Up Their Mind! $$$

XIXON SPANISH RESTAURANT
2101 Coral Way, Miami
305-854-9350
www.xixonspanishrestaurant.com
CUISINE: Spanish/Tapas Bar
DRINKS: Full Bar
SERVING: Lunch & Dinner
PRICE RANGE: $$
NEIGHBORHOOD: Shenandoah / Gables
This modern multi-level Spanish eatery featuring several rooms—a dining room, wine cellar and bakery/deli—is one of my favorite spots in the Gables. The bakery/deli & market give it a bustling feel most restaurants would die for. Food is uniformly outstanding. Large menu. Favorites: Seafood paella and Manchego. Lots of great dishes to share like fried artichokes and octopus. They get the cod from the chilly waters off Iceland.

BIZCAYA

COCONUT GROVE

While the days of Coconut Grove's ascendency in Miami is just a faded memory, there still are a few restaurants nice enough to warrant a visit.

ARIETE
3540 Main Hwy, Coconut Grove
305-640-5862
www.arietemiami.com
CUISINE: American (New)
DRINKS: Full Bar
SERVING: Dinner Tues – Sun, Lunch Sat & Sun; closed Monday
PRICE RANGE: $$$
NEIGHBORHOOD: Coconut Grove
Modern farmhouse décor (snugly arranged wooden tables) with a bar on one side of the room and an open kitchen and a wood-burning oven on the other with an ever-changing menu of American fare. Favorites: Grilled oysters, Short rib and Venison. The small plates are really small. (Too small.) By way of contrast, the Painted Hills rib eye fills the whole plate and can feed 3. Great place for weekend brunch (if you don't mind spotty service). Classic cocktails. Music tends to be intrusively loud.

BIZCAYA
The Ritz-Carlton, 3300 SW 27th Ave., Coconut Grove: 305-644-4675
www.ritzcarlton.com
CUISINE: Mediterranean

DRINKS: full bar.
SERVING: breakfast, lunch, dinner daily.
Hotel dining room. Seasonal menu with a Mediterranean twist. Especially nice is the setting: one of the most romantic open-air dining venues in Miami - complete with a lush garden cascading waterfall and candlelit tables for year-round outdoor dining. $$$-$$$$

EL CARAJO
2465 SW 17th Ave., Miami
305 856-2424
http://www.el-carajo.com
CUISINE: Spanish; tapas.
DRINKS: beer/wine.
SERVING: lunch, dinner daily.
Huge wine selection (1500 in stock). Small place, seats only 55, but good, solid food. $-$$.

GLASS & VINE
2820 McFarlane Rd., Coconut Grove,
305-200-5268
www.glassandvine.com
CUISINE: Modern American
DRINKS: Full bar
SERVING: Dinner
PRICE RANGE: $$$
NEIGHBORHOOD: Coconut Grove
Located within Peacock Park, this indoor/ outdoor eatery offers an impressive Euro-style menu.
Favorites: Watermelon salad, Skewered broccoli and Scallops, roasted lamb ribs. I'm a big fan of the iceberg wedge. But here, they take whole baby heads of Romaine and grill them with charred tomato, bacon, buttermilk and blue cheese—little bits of buckwheat replace traditional croutons. Outstanding! Intimate garden offers a great dining experience.

JAGUAR CEVICHE SPOON BAR & LATAM GRILL
3067 Grand Ave, Coconut Grove
305 444-0216
www.jaguarhg.com/restaurants
CUISINE: Latin.
DRINKS: full bar.
SERVING: lunch, dinner daily.
Ceviches served in large white ceramic spoons. Try something different: chiles en nogada, which is a dish made with poblano peppers jammed with pork and covered in a walnut-cream sauce. The Latam Grill has grilled steaks and seafood. All very nice. The meats are paired with distinctive Latin salsas. Indoor, outdoor. Casual. $$$-$$$$

LULU

3105 Commodore Plaza,
Coconut Grove: 305 447-5858
http://www.luluinthegrove.com
CUISINE: Hard to pin down.
DRINKS: full bar.
SERVING: lunch, dinner daily.
Although the menu is all over the place, it's basically an American menu with a few things (like churrasco and some pastas) thrown in to give it some variety. Nice, cozy spot right in the heart of the Grove. $$$

MONTY'S RAW BAR

2550 S. Bayshore Dr., Coconut Grove:
305-856-3992
www.montysrawbar.com
CUISINE: American.
DRINKS: full bar.
SERVING: lunch, dinner.
This joint has been here forever. Back when the Grove was "the" place to be, it was one of the hottest tickets in town. Still offers casual waterfront indoor and outdoor dining. Seafood, sandwiches, salads and ribs while listening to live music and sitting on Biscayne Bay. $$$

PANORAMA

Sonesta Bayfront Hotel,
2889 McFarlane Road, Coconut Grove
305 447-8256
http://www.sonesta.com/coconutgrove
CUISINE: Nuevo-Andean Peruvian.
DRINKS: full bar.
SERVING: breakfast, lunch, dinner
Stylish and airy contemporary setting, with floor-to-ceiling glass walls offering panoramic views of Biscayne Bay from its eighth-floor location and rooftop pool bar.

KEY BISCAYNE

If you find yourself on the Key, as we call it here in Miami, you could do worse than to drop into one of these nice eateries.

EL GRAN INKA

606 Crandon Blvd., Key Biscayne
305 365-7883
http://www.graninka.com
CUISINE: Peruvian.
DRINKS: full bar.
SERVING: lunch, dinner.
You'd never know this was a chain (they have outlets in Guatemala, El Salvador, Costa Rica, but in the USA, they are only in Miami in 3 locations). Really good Peruvian food. This is an upscale place, but there are other places you can get great Peruvian food (see Chalon's on South Beach) for a quarter the price point. $$$$

LIGHTHOUSE CAFÉ

1200 Crandon Blvd., Key Biscayne, 305-361-8487
www.lighthouserestaurants.com
CUISINE: Cafes
DRINKS: No Booze
SERVING: Breakfast-Lunch
PRICE RANGE: $$
NEIGHBORHOOD: Key Biscayne
Completely open-air eatery in Bill Bagg's Cape Florida State Park, so make sure the weather's to your liking. Has a large menu, salads, sandwiches, pastas and some Cuban dishes (like pork chunks and black bean soup).There's a small fee to enter the park.

NOVECENTO

620 Crandon Blvd., Key Biscayne 305 362-0900
http://www.novecento.com
CUISINE: Argentine steakhouse.
DRINKS: full bar.
SERVING: lunch, dinner.
Although to me this is basically an Argentine steakhouse (and it's really good), they say it's not just Argentine, but also Mediterranean and Pan Latin highlighted by French techniques. That the cuisine is not a fusion; rather each style is separate and is a pure reflection of its heritage. But to me, it's still an Argentine steakhouse. Indoor, outdoor.

RUSTY PELICAN

3201 Rickenbacker Causeway, Key Biscayne: 305 361-3818
www.therustypelican.com
CUISINE: American; seafood.
DRINKS: full bar.
SERVING: lunch, dinner daily.
Heavy on the seafood dishes, but what you really come here for is the spectacular view of downtown Miami. It's got an off-putting "corporate" feel to it and is huge (seats 400, but can do parties for 1,000). I always go on "off" days, and wouldn't be caught dead here on a Friday or Saturday night. But I know many people who love it when it's jammed. It's great for either lunch or dinner, depending on whether you want to look at the view in sunny daylight or romantic evenings. I even like it here on rainy, gusty days because I like looking out over the water when it's stormy. $$$

WHISKEY JOE'S BAR & GRILL

3301 Rickenbacker Cswy., Key Biscayne: 305-423-6590
www.whiskeyjoestampa.com/
CUISINE: American
DRINKS: Full Bar
SERVING: Lunch, Dinner
An offshoot of the original Tampa bar & grill, this location has a Key West vibe serving everything from crab cake sliders to mango salad with coconut shrimp. Live music. $$

Chapter 4
NIGHTLIFE

SOUTH BEACH

A night on the town means different things to different people: some people want to go to a nightclub, spend $300 for bottle service. For someone else, it's a stroll on the beach.

HOTEL LOBBY BARS
SOUTH BEACH

Most tourists usually only see the lobby of the hotel they're in. Unless a nightclub or lounge (like **Wall** in the **W**) is located in a hotel, they don't see other hotel lobbies.

Or—more to the point here—the bars in or off the lobbies that can be worth a trip in and of themselves.

One of the things I like to do when I'm entertaining out-of-towners is to take them on a **Hotel Lobby Bar Tour**. The idea is simple: select a list of four or five or six hotels and spend the evening moving from one to the other. Have a single drink in each, maybe an appetizer or two if you're peckish, and then get out and go on to the next one. You'll have had one of the best evenings of your visit. And you'll absorb quite a visual education on the glories of architectural design on South Beach—all for the (sometimes hefty) price of a drink.

It's essential to appreciate what the South Beach lobby bars are like (for comparison's sake) to make a short excursion (a ten-minute cab ride) up to the **Eden Roc** and the **Fontainebleau**, hotels next door to each other, both designed by the legendary architect

Morris Lapidus, the man who once said, "Too much is never enough."

Walk through the lobby of the Fontainebleau first. It's quite expansive. Have a drink and then walk next door to the Eden Roc. These lobbies are stunning.

Then come back to South Beach and see what other designers have done to fully appreciate the over-the-top genius of Morris Lapidus.

AC HOTEL MIAMI BEACH
2912 Collins Ave, Miami Beach
786-264-4720
www.marriott.com/hotels/travel/miaac-ac-hotel-miami-beach
Located a bit north of South Beach, this hotel, like so many South Beach hotels, offers a great lounge with a happening bar scene. Bar offers a menu of local craft beer, wine on tap, creative cocktails and a bar menu of curated tapas.

THE DELANO
1685 Collins Ave., Miami Beach
305-672-2000
www.delano-hotel.com
Enjoy the whimsical design brilliance of **Philippe Starck** as you walk through the lobby to the **Rose Bar**. When you get a load of his lobby interior here, you will understand the profound impact he has had on design around the world, and all the copycats that have mimicked his ideas. But I credit hotelier **Ian Schrager** for being even smarter and more talented than Starck: he hired him! Both Schrager and Starck have moved on from the Delano long ago, but their influence remains here to be seen and appreciated.

MONDRIAN
1100 West Ave., Miami Beach
305-514-1500
www.mondrian-miami.com
Here you'll get a full sense of how strong Starck's influence is. Here it's all white, white and whiter. There's a stunning indoor bar, and this as well as the restaurant overlook the pool and Biscayne Bay. Outdoor bar as well. This is "Sunset Central," as it's the only hotel besides the Standard that faces west.

THE SAGAMORE
1671 Collins Ave., Miami Beach

W SOUTH BEACH

305-535-8088
www.sagamorehotel.com
With 93 suites and two-story bungalows, the Sagamore is a bit big for a "boutique" hotel (though to be fair it does possess a boutique hotel's attention to service and detail). Not in question, however, is the inn's designation as an "Art Hotel."

THE SETAI
2001 Collins Ave., Miami Beach
305-520-6000
www.thesetaihotel.com
The front half of this uber luxury inn is the '30s era Dempsey Vanderbilt Hotel; the remainder is a modern glass tower that reaches up past the imagination. When you enter the lobby bar in this place you leave South Beach behind and move into whole other dimension.

W SOUTH BEACH
2201 Collins Ave., Miami Beach
305-938-3000
www.wsouthbeach.com
The Living Room Bar off the lobby will give you an idea of what the big money buys in terms of design today. Expect this place to be busy, because it's the Hot Spot this year. If you're going for dinner, let the trendsetters trip over themselves at **Mr. Chow** while you go to **Solea**, one of the best true Spanish restaurants in town. Also home to the uber-hip bottle club lounge, **Wall**.

THE VICTOR
1144 Ocean Dr., Miami Beach
305-428-1234
www.hotelvictorsouthbeach.com
If you must hit Ocean Drive, then this is the place. Designed by the famed L. Murray Dixon in 1937 and retrofit by Parisian Jacques Garcia back in 2003 (to the reported tune of $48 million), the Victor's got both a charming lobby bar (V Bar) and a beautiful pool-with-a-view (Vue). And if you close your eyes you're on a classic ocean liner, and South Beach is as wondrous as ever. Take special note of the restored mural in the lobby.

NIGHTCLUBS
SOUTH BEACH

BASEMENT
2901 Collins Ave, Miami Beach
786-257-4548
www.basementmiami.com
Located in the basement of **The Edition**, one of Miami Beach's hottest new hotels, this unique club was developed by Ian Schrager of Studio 54 offering music from Miami veteran Ben Pundole. A gathering spot for hipsters and those who aspire to be cool. Dress the part.

BODEGA TAQUERIA Y TEQUILA
1220 16th St, Miami Beach
305-704-2145
www.bodegasouthbeach.com
Some come for the great Mexican street food (I come here with a Mexican who says the tacos are the best) but others come for the great bar scene located behind the door that looks like it leads to a port-a-potty. It actually leads down a short hallway to one of the hippest bars in Miami. This bar offers a relaxed atmosphere with friendly bartenders (a rarity these days) serving creative cocktails. Velvet couches, unique art, and a chill balcony. Pool table, DJs, and rowdy crowd, most of them with more tattoos than I care to see, but the place is happening. I take visitors here, but it's not a place for an old fart like me to hang out.

LIV
Fontainebleau, 4441 Collins Ave., Miami Beach: 305-674-4680
www.livnightclub.com/
The Fontainebleau's signature hotspot may need no introduction, especially if you're familiar with the likes of **Tiesto** and **Cedric Gervais**. But wall-to-wall weekends of world-class DJs is only one of the reasons to trek up Collins and join the madding crowd; the other is

Wednesday night's **Dirty Harry** party, which pits Miami's best spinners with some of the world's most out-there performers. Sure, it'll cost you. But some wild nights are well worth paying for.

NIKKI BEACH CLUB
1 Ocean Dr., Miami Beach
305-538-1111
www.nikkibeach.com
What started out here at the foot of Ocean Drive now has outposts in places like Cabo San Lucas, Marbella, Cannes and all around the world. Full list of activities, but it's still a great place to lounge in the sun or play at night. And you're right on the beach, perfect for that nighttime walk with a moon over Miami. Dancing.

STORY
136 Collins Ave., Miami Beach
305-538-2424
www.storymiami.com
I remember very well the nightclub Amnesia that once occupied this enormous space. Three levels of madness, all of it driven by heart-thumping music. Another outpost where $20 buys you a vodka cran.

BARS & LOUNGES
SOUTH BEACH

B BAR
1440 Ocean Dr., Miami Beach
305-531-6100
www.thebetsyhotel.com
Designed by Chi-town power broker **Callin Fortis**, of Big Time Design Studios, the very same cat who brought the wild world everything Crobar to Exit 66, B Bar is the Betsy's basement playroom par excellence. And at equal parts speakeasy and hide-out, it's one of the damn few good reasons even to dare Ocean Drive anymore.

BROKEN SHAKER
Freehand Hotel, 2727 Indian Creek Dr, Miami Beach, 305-531-2727
www.thefreehand.com
Located in the backyard of the Freehand Hotel, formerly the Indian Creek Hotel, that has now been transformed into a hostel. Here you'll find the hostel's pool, herb garden, bocce ball court, ping pong tables and outdoor seating area. The crowd is friendly and there's often live music. Small menu available.

THE CATALINA HOTEL & BEACH CLUB
1732 Collins Ave., Miami Beach
305-674-1160
www.catalinasouthbeach.com
Over the past couple years, the Catalina has turned into a sorta adult amusement park in its own right. There are the joints: **Maxine's Bistro**, **Kung Fu Kitchen** and **Sushi, Red Bar**. There are the pools: Bamboo and Rooftop. And then there's the Bridge – now Verge – Art Fair, which takes place each year at **Art Basel**. All in all, it's a charming antidote to the mega-inns. And downright affordable to boot.

KILL YOUR IDOL
222 Espanola Way, Miami Beach
305-672-1852
www.killyouridol.com
Packed with pop culture artifacts such as a Playboy pinball machine and a life-sized Bruce Lee, this sleek little hang would be just what the locals ordered if she or he had any

say in the matter. Drinks are less than cheap, and if you're hungry you can even grab food from The Alibi. And don't forget to drop a dime in that jukebox. DJ Smeejay is often seen bouncing the club in late hours.

LIVING ROOM - W HOTEL
2201 Collins Ave, Miami Beach
305-938-3000
www.wsouthbeach.com/living-room-bar
Located in the lobby of W Hotel South Beach, this bar specializes in custom made cocktails filled with natural ingredients like fruits, herbs, & edible flowers. The drink menu features infused, molecular mixology, and innovative concoctions like the Electric Watermelon (made with fresh watermelon, rosemary honey, peach bitters, and bourbon then topped with honeydew caviar). Drinks are pricey.

© Ernesto Sampoli

MOKAI
235 - 23rd St., Miami Beach
786-735-3322
www.mokaimiami.com/
Now owned by The Opium Group, Mokai still retains some of its storied hedonism. It just has a different accent.

MYNT
1921 Collins Ave., Miami Beach
305-532-0727
www.myntlounge.com
Hot club serving locals and an international clientele. Big stars come here: Mickey Rourke, Sean Penn, Jennifer Lopez, Cameron Diaz, Britney Spears, Ricky Martin, Jamie Foxx, Colin Farrell.

PURDY LOUNGE
1811 Purdy Ave., Miami Beach
305-531-4622
http://www.purdylounge.com/
Another youngish hangout, this driven by different DJs and ranked #18 on **World's Best Bars Top 100**. The long-running Chocolate Sundays remains the best bet. Some of the better local pool players shark around the shadows of this bar's pool table.

REGENT COCKTAIL CLUB
1690 Collins Ave, Miami Beach
786-975-2555
www.galehotel.com/nightlife/regent-cocktail-club
Located in the newly renovated Gale Hotel, the 1940s décor gives this place a speakeasy feel but make no mistake the cocktails are modern. You know the drinks are good here because the head mixologist was featured on the cover of GQ. Everything old is hip again at this new bar. Lite-bite menu available.

ROCKWELL
743 Washington Ave, Miami Beach
305-793-3882
http://rockwellmiami.com/
This hip spot is the brainchild of former Liquid nightclub owner Chris Paciello and is the hangout for celebs like Justin Bieber and Sean Combs when they're in town.

SING SING KARAOKE
717 Washington Ave, Miami Beach
305-763-8410
www.singsingmiami.com
This bar and lounge serves up the Karaoke experience like no other local venue. Book a private room or take the stage in the main room.

SKYBAR
Shore Club
1901 Collins Ave., Miami Beach
305-695-3100
www.shoreclub.com
Out by the pool you'll find the still-hot Skybar. Lots of celebs and heavy lifters.

DIVE BARS
SOUTH BEACH

Well, there used to be a lot more of **these** (does anyone remember **Jessie's Dollhouse Bar** on Washington Avenue?), but gentrification and soaring rents have squeezed a lot of colorful joints out of business. But a few remain.

MAC'S CLUB DEUCE

MAC'S CLUB DEUCE

222 14th St. (between Collins & Washington), Miami Beach
305-531-6200
No web site, and certainly doesn't need one

The legendary dive bar where many scenes in "Miami Vice" were shot. The neon the crew put in was so cool owner **Mac Klein** left it up. (Mac celebrated his 100th birthday in 2015 and I was there. He died a year later at 101.) In this dive, which his family still operates the way Mac did, Happy Hour starts at 8 (ahem, that's 8 a.m., and runs till 7 p.m.). Regular patron "Persian Jimmy" used to say: "If you can't get drunk in eleven hours, you're not tryin'." A must visit. Buy a T-shirt.

FINNEGAN'S 2

942 Lincoln Rd., Miami Beach
305-538-7997
www.finnegansbars.com
WEBSITE DOWN AT PRESS TIME.

Sports bar with lots of TVs. Pub fare. Low prices. The only real dive bar on Lincoln Road. ☹
I used to think the food here was awful, but I got stuck there one night in the rain and the chicken wings and French fries were to die for!

RADIO BAR
814 – 1st St., Miami Beach
305-397-8382
www.radiosouthbeach.com
The most unlikely dive bar populated by surfers and skateboarders. Its tony neighbors include Joe's Stone Crab and Smith & Wollensky. Go figure.

TED'S HIDEAWAY
124 Second St., Miami Beach
305-532-9869
https://m.mainstreethub.com/index.php/tedshideaway
A dive bar where you can find pool tables, beer and booze and girl bartenders from places like Romania, Russia, Bulgaria. A little sandier than the **Deuce**, and a little shadier too. So what? Open daily 8am-5am.

GAY BARS / CLUBS

SOUTH BEACH

Gone are the days when the big gay clubs provided that indefinable spark that ignited the South Beach nightlife scene and made it explode. The best "gay" clubs (**Warsaw Ballroom**—it ran from 1989 to 1998 and **Paragon**, from March 1992 to 1994, attracted a heady mix of gay **and** straight people, but they were all people "on the edge," at the forefront of whatever was happening. Add to this mix that the White Party was the first and most lavish party among the international gay **Circuit parties**, and you had a combustible environment.

It's waaaay different now. The cover at the Warsaw was $5. There was a tiny VIP Room upstairs. But mostly anybody could get into it. Money didn't matter. No bottle service. No attitude.

The reputation that South Beach is a huge gay Mecca lingers on and can't be shaken. But there's actually only a handful of gay bars on South Beach.

GAYTHERING
1409 Lincoln Rd, Miami Beach
786-284-1176 www.gaythering.com
This bar is located in the cozy lobby of Miami Beach's only "straight friendly" hotel. Located where trendy Lincoln Road meets Biscayne Bay. It's a sleek bar with a friendly staff, craft cocktails, upscale ambience.

SCORE

SCORE

1437 Washington Ave.
(at Espanola Way), Miami Beach,
305-535-1111.
www.scorebar.net

For many years located on Lincoln Road, Score moved in 2013 to the club space formerly known as Liquid. This large bar, lounge, dance club has been wowing the gay crowd for years. **Lady Gaga** performed here in 2009 before she was famous. (Maybe that's what **made** her famous!) Usually has a cover charge after 10.

TWIST

1057 Washington Ave., Miami Beach:
305-538-9478.
www.twistsobe.com/

South Beach's famous long-running gay bar, where everybody goes after 3 a.m. to revel in what's left of the old decadence. (This is where the staffs of the other gays bars end up between 3 and 5 a.m.) They might have called this place the Last Chance Saloon because if you can't pick up someone here, you're really not trying very hard.

SPACE

THE MAINLAND

NIGHTCLUBS MAINLAND

CHURCHILL'S PUB

5501 NE 2nd Ave., Miami
305-757-1807
http://churchillspub.com

Up in Little Haiti, this joint (and it **is** a joint) offers live underground music. Been here since 1979. Indie music is the scene here.

EL PALENQUE NIGHTCLUB

1115 NW 22nd Ave., Miami
305-644-7376
No web site at presstime

Well-known Mexican bands featured monthly. Other weekends, DJ Turko mans the turntables, playing bachata, salsa, and merengue on Fridays, open format on Saturdays, and primarily Mexican music on Sundays. Nightly, a sexy dance contest. Patrons vote on the girl with the best presentation. 5 beers for $18. Also bar food. Sometimes a cover, depending on entertainment.

SPACE
34 NE 11th St., Miami
786-357-6456
http://clubspace.com
Big-time DJs and dancing is the scene here in this massive club. For the hard partying set.

BARS & LOUNGES MAINLAND

THE ANDERSON MIAMI
709 NE 79th St., Miami
305-757-3368
www.theandersonmiami.com
Located right off Biscayne Blvd, this hipster hangout (formerly Magnum's) is a combination of indoor and outdoor areas. The inside features a long dark bar area with great music and even a menu of snacks (from Fried chicken sandwich to TexMex). This new interpretation of an old theme offers a cleaner, hipper party atmosphere but the piano and dance floor remain.

THE BAR AT 1306
1306 N. Miami Ave., Miami
305-377-2277
www.1306miami.com
Small bar that serves up great crafted cocktails with a nice selection of tunes. Note that this dimly lit place is intimate (about 5 barstools, couple of couches and a few tables) but friendly. This place is developed by the same owners of the former Grand Central so expect a good time.

THE BAR AT LEVEL 25
Conrad Hotel
1395 Brickell Ave., Miami
305-503-6529
http://conradhotels1.hilton.com
Level 25 indicates that this bar is on the 25th floor, and worth a trip just to get a gander at the stunning view from this height. Best time to go is weekday happy-hour when prices drop to a reasonable $5 to $8. Later, prices go way up. Free valet parking (at least). Food served all day and night. (Try the tempura-battered soft-shell crab with spicy chipotle aioli.)

THE BAR NEXT DOOR

2531 NW Second Ave., Miami
305-748-2828
www.woodtavernmiami.com
This place is the personification of cool with graffiti on the ceiling and stained-glass lighting fixtures. Hipsters and locals fill this place for the great selection of beer and craft cocktails. Bar menu offers basics like hamburgers, short rib sandwiches and wings. Indoor & outdoor seating.

BLACKBIRD ORDINARY

729 SW 1st Ave, Miami
305-671-3307
www.blackbirdordinary.com
Located in Brickell, this hipster lounge features live music and a relaxed atmosphere. This is not just a bar but a scene and the crowd wanders inside and out. There are even board games if you get bored. Friendly crowd and delicious cocktails. If you're looking for a quiet spot this isn't it.

BLUE MARTINI

900 S Miami Ave #250, Miami
305-981-2583
http://bluemartinilounge.com
42 versions of the martini. This spot fills up with yuppies from nearby Brickell Avenue offices, but still a good-looking crowd. No one here didn't go to college. The servers are young and attractive, the bar food better than average. In Mary Brickell Village downtown. Happy hour specials; cover charge (if you can believe it) Friday and Saturday nights.

CHURCHILL'S PUB

5501 NE 2nd Ave., Miami
305-757-1807
www.churchillspub.com
Place in Little Haiti that was here (from 1979) **before** there was a Little Haiti. Little Haiti just sort of grew up around Churchill's. I always find it funny to go over here, walk into the place, and find **white** people. Big supporter of the indie music scene, punk rock, etc.

THE CORNER
1035 N Miami Ave, Miami
305-961-7887
www.thecornermiami.com
Located in downtown's entertainment district (next door to Club Space), this charming nightspot offers a variety of interesting cocktails that you won't find next door. Here you'll find a modern-day saloon atmosphere and cocktails served with natural ingredients. This bar also boasts a nice selection of craft beers on draft, a price-conscious wine list and an impressive late-night menu.

EL PATIO WYNWOOD
167 NW 23 St, Miami, 786-409-2241
www.elpatiowynwood.com
Outdoor spot that is definitely part of the scene. Great specials (4 beers for $4? Bring it on). Lots of seating but it's all outdoors. Some of it is covered – some not. Nice selection of beers and crafted cocktails. Variety of tunes play depending on the DJ. Live bands usually play Latin music.

ELECTRIC PICKLE
2826 N Miami Ave., Miami
305-456-5613
www.electricpicklemiami.com
Wide variety of music is played here, from electronica to hip hop, Caribbean sounds, etc. It's a small room in the emerging **Wynwood District**. (My office is a block away.)

VAGABOND HOTEL LOUNGE/BAR
7301 Biscayne Blvd, Miami
305-400-8420
www.thevagabondhotel.com
Step back in time at relive the old Miami experience at the reopened Vagabond Hotel. This is one of my favorite spots in Miami. Lounge by the poolside bar – a mix of vintage Miami and Palm Springs. Great happy hour on weekends and affordable cocktails. (The restaurant is really good, too.)

GAY BARS & LOUNGES MAINLAND

JAMBOREE LOUNGE
7005 Biscayne Blvd., Miami
305-759-3413
Sleazy gay dive bar.

Chapter 5
ATTRACTIONS

COUNTY BEACHES

SOUTH BEACH ATTRACTIONS

MUSEUMS

MAINLAND ATTRACTIONS / TOURS

THE BEACHES

You did come here for the beaches, right? Well, assuming you did, you have to know there **are** other beaches besides South Beach, thank you very much. Here are my favorites:

BAL HARBOUR BEACH

Collins Ave. - 96th St. to Haulover Inlet, Bal Harbour: 305/947-3525
www.BalHarbourFlorida.com
Palm-shaded jogging path curves around mile-long beach. Jetty (with fishing permitted) at north end of beach. Limited metered parking lot available beneath Haulover Bridge. No lifeguards or showers.

BILL BAGGS CAPE FLORIDA STATE BEACH

1200 S. Crandon Blvd., Key Biscayne: 305/361-5811
http://www.FloridaStateParks.org
A very scenic beach at the southern tip of Key Biscayne. Walking and bicycle trails wind through native vegetation. Historic lighthouse and food concession. Restrooms, picnic tables and shower facilities available. Parking fee.

CRANDON PARK BEACH

4000 Crandon Blvd., Key Biscayne: 305/361-5421
www.miamidade.gov/parks/parks/crandon_beach.asp
Three-mile long lagoon style beach protected by 13 lifeguard towers. Beach wheelchairs for rent. Children's carrousel, playgrounds and picnic areas. Ideal for families. Shower facilities, restrooms, shelters and lifeguards. Parking fee.

HAULOVER BEACH PARK / NUDE BEACH / GAY NUDE BEACH

10800 Collins Ave., Miami Beach: 305/947-3525
www.hauloverbeach.org
Spacious beach with shady picnic area/ barbecue grills near the dunes. Beach wheelchairs for rent. Pedestrian tunnels link to the park and marina on Biscayne Bay. Nine-hole golf course, tennis courts, kite flying area and kite shop. Clothing-optional section at northern end, with the gay section farthest north. Parking fee.

MIAMI BEACH/ SOUTH POINTE PARK

Ocean Dr. at 5th St., Miami Beach: 305/673-7779
www.miamibeachfl.gov
Entrance through the park at 1 Washington Ave. Beach located at the southern tip of South Beach. Great place to watch cruise ships sailing out to sea. Parking fee.

MIAMI BEACH – SOUTH BEACH

Ocean Drive & 5th St. to Collins Ave. & 21st St., Miami Beach
305/673-7714
www.miamibeachfl.gov
Entrance anywhere there is a public access walkway.

MIAMI BEACH – CENTRAL

Collins Ave. - 21st St. to 46th St., Miami Beach: 305/673-7714
www.miamibeachfl.gov
Raised boardwalk over the dunes popular for strolling and jogging. Proximity to sidewalk cafes along Collins Avenue. Lifeguard towers, food/drink concessions, beach chair/umbrella rentals. Parking fee.

SURFSIDE BEACH

Collins Ave. from 88th St. to 96th St., Surfside
www.townofsurfsidefl.gov
Facilities are available in 93rd St. Community Center for fee.

VIRGINIA KEY BEACH – NORTH

North of Rickenbacker Cswy. At Crandon Blvd., Key Biscayne
305/575-5256
www.virginiakeybeachpark.net
Windsurfing and ultra light seaplane rental. Great views of Brickell Avenue and downtown Miami skyline. Food/drink concessions, restroom. Parking fee.

VIRGINIA KEY BEACH – SOUTH

South of Rickenbacker Causeway, Key Biscayne: 305/361-2833
www.virginiakeybeachpark.net
Ultra-secluded beach close to Key Biscayne. Shady areas, nature trails and a bird sanctuary nearby. Only beach in Miami-Dade County where dogs on leashes are allowed.

SOUTH BEACH ATTRACTIONS

FOR THE TOURIST

A few suggestions to keep you busy when you're not at the beach, not in a club, not in a restaurant and not shopping:

SPECIFIC INFORMATION DURING YOUR VISIT. Check out the listings in the weekly newspaper **New Times**, which has boxes on every corner, or use your laptop (or increasingly these days, even

ART DECO DISTRICT

your cellphone) and go to their web site, www.miaminewtimes.com. The **Miami Herald** only has a good list in its Friday edition. But they also have comprehensive listings online at www.miamiherald.com.

ART DECO TOURS

South Beach Art Deco District
305-814-4058
www.artdecotours.com
Enrich your visit to South Beach with an enlightening walking tour of the famed Art Deco district. Transport in time to the '20's, '30's and beyond. Learn about the colorful history and admire unique architecture and design with exclusive access to interiors and rooftops. Tours great for families. Other tours available: Little Havana and Art Deco Cocktail Tour – historical tour with cocktails.

CHAMBER OF COMMERCE

1920 Meridian Ave., Miami Beach
305-674-1300.
www.miamibeachchamber.com
Has lots of listings on its web site to help you plan your trip.

OFFICIAL ART DECO GIFT SHOP & WALKING TOURS

10th Street & Ocean Dr., Miami Beach: 305-531-3484 Also: 305-672-2014. Organized by the Miami Design Preservation League
www.mdpl.org
They have a very interesting 90-minute walking tour that provides an introduction to the Art Deco, Mediterranean Revival, and Miami Modern (MiMo) styles found within the Miami Beach Architectural Historic District. Explore hotels, restaurants, and other commercial structures with a visit to a number of interiors. Tours depart from the Art Deco

Gift Shop on the following schedule: Daily at 10:30am (except Thursday, 6:30pm). Reservation not needed. Just show up at the Art Deco Gift Shop 10 minutes of the scheduled departure time in order to purchase your ticket, $20. (Verify this by phone before you go.)

BIKE RENTALS & TOURS

210 – 10th St. (Collins Ave. and 10th St.), Miami Beach: 305-604-0001 / www.bikeandroll.com

CITI BIKE (Bike Rentals)

723 Washington Ave., Miami Beach
305-532-9494
www.citibikemiami.com

The **Citi Bike** program is operated by DECOBIKE and is **Miami's** bike sharing and rental system.

BOTANICAL GARDENS

2000 Convention Center Dr., Miami Beach: 305-673-7256
www.mbgarden.org.

A restful place (OK, it's a little dull) in a very un-restful city, tucked ingloriously in a nook between the parking lot adjacent to the Convention Center and the Dade Canal marking the northernmost point of South Beach. A three-minute walk north of Lincoln Road.

COLONY THEATRE

1040 Lincoln Rd., Miami Beach
305-674-1040
www.colonytheatremiamibeach.com

Check to see exactly what's playing in this little Art Deco theatre on Lincoln Road. It's an architectural gem inside and out.

DUCK (WATER & LAND) TOURS

1661 James Ave., Miami Beach
305-673-2217
www.ducktoursmiami.com

Leaving from the heart of South Beach, these amphibious vehicles provide a once in a lifetime journey (90 minutes) of the famous Miami landmarks before a dramatic "Splashdown" into Biscayne Bay for a close up look at the many homes of the "Rich & Famous" on Star Island. Soon after your journey on a Miami Duck Tour begins, you will quickly realize that you are engaged in an interactive performance that far exceeds your standard tour expectations. Each tour guide has a background in acting/comedy to ensure a highly entertaining experience for each passenger complete with jokes, music, plenty of interaction and of course "quacking." Don't let all of that joking around fool you; each guide at Miami Duck Tours takes their knowledge of the Magic City very seriously. (I took this from their web site. I've never actually been on this little trip.)

ESPAÑOLA WAY

Española Way is quaintly referred to by tourism officials as "a historic Spanish village" (actually, it's a single street located in the area bounded by 14th and 15th Streets and Washington and Jefferson avenues on South Beach. The street has recently reopened after a $2.5 million restoration.). But it's still worth strolling down and having lunch or dinner. For South Beach, it really is quaint. With Mediterranean Revival buildings dating back to the 1920s

FILLMORE AT THE GLEASON THEATRE

1700 Convention Center Dr., Miami Beach: 305-673-7300.
http://fillmoremb.com/

ESPAÑOLA WAY

FISHING

300 Alton Rd., Miami Beach Marina
305-372-9470
www.therewardfleet.com

They have a big boat that takes a crowd out to go fishing. But they also act as booking agents for many charter boats, skiff guides, flats guides and back country guides. Give them a call with what you are looking for and they'll get it done for you. They can also arrange sightseeing. They have the only blue water sightseeing vessel for up to 103 passengers in South Florida.

KAYAK RENTALS & TOURS

1771 Purdy Ave., Miami Beach
305-975-5087
www.southbeachkayak.com/

It's a little tough to find this place. It's tucked away over on the last road before you cross the Venetian Causeway next door to the old Joe Allen's (now **PB Steak**) restaurant. But it's right across the street from the Sunset Harbour Marina so you can slip into the water very quickly.

LINCOLN ROAD

www.lincolnroad.org

As Ocean Drive has become more "touristy," Lincoln Road has taken up the slack as a place more frequented by locals. The web site has all the stores, shops, restaurants. The architect that created the Fontainebleau and the Eden Roc (Morris Lapidus), conjured up the fanciful shapes strewn along the center of Lincoln Road. They are worth a second look as you move down the street.

MIAMI BEACH GOLF CLUB

2301 Alton Rd., Miami Beach
305-532-3350
www.miamibeachgolfclub.com

Originally opened as Bayshore Golf Course in 1923 as part of pioneering developer Carl Fisher's ambitious Alton Beach subdivision that was designed to lure wealthy winter residents from New York, Indianapolis and Detroit, this professional course is now owned by the city.

MIAMI CITY BALLET
2200 Liberty Ave., Miami Beach
305-929-7000
www.miamicityballet.org.
One of America's most acclaimed ballet companies. If you're in town when they are performing, you owe it to yourself to spend an evening with them.

NEW WORLD SYMPHONY
500 – 17th St., Miami Beach
305-673-3330 www.nws.edu
NWS, America's "orchestra academy," is housed in a stunning new (2011) Frank Gehry-designed concert hall at the corner of 17th Street and Washington Avenue, just north of Lincoln Road. Students from NWS leave to populate the great orchestras all over the world. Try to work in a concert if you're in town during their season, because it's a real treat you won't find anywhere else in the world (and you get a good look inside Gehry's new architectural wonder).

SOUTH FLORIDA ART CENTER
924 Lincoln Rd., Miami Beach
305-674-8278
www.artcentersf.org
The buildings housing SFAC have been converted into a warren of tiny studios where several dozen artists working on all media do their thing. Artists you'd never get to see (because the rents are so high on Lincoln Road) get to show their wares, and you get to watch them paint, watch them sculpt, meet them, and if you like what you see, even buy their work. Definitely worth a walk-through.

SOUTH POINTE PARK
1 Washington Ave., Miami Beach
305-673-7779
http://web.miamibeachfl.gov/
At the very southern tip of Miami Beach overlooking Government Cut, the inlet leading to the Port of Miami. Great place to go on Friday or Saturday afternoons to watch the cruise ships head out in a stately procession as they begin their trips to the Caribbean. Only problem with this place: after spending millions "improving" this park, they removed **every single shade tree** from the western half of the park, so it's unbearably hot half the year. Very inhospitable place. You don't know whether to shoot the talentless designers or the incredibly incompetent city planning officials who approved this abortion.

TOURIST HOTLINE: 305-673-7400. Can usually steer you in the right direction.

THE VILLA CASA CASUARINA (Versace Mansion)
1114 Ocean Dr., Miami Beach
786-485-2200
www.vmmiamibeach.com
Poor Peter Loftin. Well, not exactly "poor" Peter Loftin. He's the North Carolina gazillionaire who bought the villa on Ocean Drive where Versace was notoriously gunned down by Andrew Cunanan. He's turned it into a private club, a hotel, an events location, but nothing worked. Finally, in 2013, he sold it to the family that owns the Jordache fashion line. (Has anyone noticed the irony?) What they ought to do is turn it into a museum, so people could go inside to see how Versace lived. I've been to many events and dinners inside, and it's quite the little pleasure palace. He lived well. Currently The Villa Casa Casuarina is open as an upscale hotel and the restaurant is open to the public.

CASA CASUARINA (VERSACE MANSION)

WATER TOURS
OCEAN FORCE ADVENTURES
Miami Beach Marina, 300 Alton Rd., Miami Beach: 305-372-3388
www.Oceanforceadventures.com.
Experience the excitement of a Zodiac RIB ride (these are the same boats used by the FBI, special military forces, DEA and Coast Guard) on their 2-hour outdoor adventure sightseeing boat tours as you speed across brilliant blue ocean waters and soak up the sun-drenched Florida skies to explore the glamour, the mystery and the history of Miami Beach and Biscayne Bay. Their boat is docked at the center dock directly behind the main entrance to the marina.

CRUISE SHIP DEPARTURE SPECTACLE
Although it's not what you'd call an official "attraction," it's still one of the best things to do if you're visiting South Beach on a Friday or Saturday. These are the two days the ocean liners head out to the Caribbean with their boatloads of people who sail right by South Beach without ever knowing what they're missing. You get a pretty good view of exclusive Fisher Island across the Cut and the ferries that take cars and people over there. If you don't mind spending a few bucks (well, quite a few bucks), go early (say, 4pm) and get a table outside at **Smith and Wollensky's** and have their fabulous cold seafood platter or one of their great steaks and watch as the ships go by. Or just nurse a drink at the bar and you'll get the same experience without the high cost. If you're really broke, sit on the rocks under the shade of the seagrape trees hugging the Cut and enjoy it all for free!

HOTEL LOBBY TOUR
See the opening section of the **Nightlife** chapter for a rundown on my favorite hotel lobbies.

WOLFSONIAN MUSEUM

MUSEUMS

WOLFSONIAN MUSEUM
1001 Washington Ave., Miami Beach:
305-531-1001
www.wolfsonian.org
One of the most unusual museums in the world, it was founded by the mercurial millionaire Micky Wolfson. His fascinating collection of objects from the modern era (1885-1945) focuses on how art and design shape and reflect the human experience. Some of the things Mickey collected you won't believe. (Ask them where the toasters are.) Florida Int'l University now operates the museum. There's even a little café in here that's quite a find and worth a trip on its own. Free museum tours every Friday evening at 6 p.m.

HOLOCAUST MEMORIAL
1933 Meridian Ave., Miami Beach
305-538-1663
www.holocaustmmb.org
Right behind the Botanical Gardens, across from the same parking lot, you'll find this poignant memorial to the Holocaust. Don't rush through this open-air exhibit. (Chamber of Commerce is across the street where you can grab stacks of brochures.)

WORLD EROTIC ART MUSEUM
1205 Washington Ave., Miami Beach:
305-532-9336
www.weam.com
All the kinds of forbidden art previously hidden from public view. (Well, until the Internet came along.) Honestly, this place sounds like something so tacky you'd never give it a second thought, but I was finally persuaded to visit the place, and it has thousands of museum-quality items

that will really impress you. My reaction to the world-class collection assembled here is exactly the opposite of what I imagined it would be. So, give it a shot.

JEWISH MUSEUM OF FLORIDA

301 Washington Ave., Miami Beach
305-672-5044
www.jewishmuseum.com
Unique destination for people of every age and background. Site comprised of two former synagogues, on the National Register of Historic Places, restored by the Museum, and connected with a glass-domed bistro. Core exhibit, **MOSAIC**, depicts 250 years of Jewish Life in Florida, a story of one immigrant group that is generic for all families. Enjoy at least two more changing history or art exhibits, films and their Museum Store. Museum open 10-5 Tuesdays-Sundays, closed Civil & Jewish Holidays; free on Saturdays. Wheelchair accessible and parking in vicinity.

ART TOURS

Ever since **Art Basel** selected South Beach for its Western Hemisphere art fair (instead of, say, someplace sensible like New York), all of Miami has become an international hub of artistic activity. And the really big money rolls into town the first of December to buy and sell. And it's big, Big, BIG!

And it's all of Miami, not just South Beach. The frenzied activity has poured across the causeways to Miami's Wynwood and Design districts, full of mostly empty warehouses anyway, with developers begging for something to happen in a moribund and speculative economy.

Developers like **Craig Robins, Tony Goldman** and **Martin Margulies** opened HUGE warehouses and collected art themselves with wild abandon. (This was during that period when anybody with money began collecting art because it was fashionable, not because the "art" was necessarily any good.)

So the town was ripe for a cataclysmic shake up.

Art Basel in Miami has become the most interesting and exciting art fair in the world in just a few short years, easily eclipsing its sponsor and eponymous creator, Art Basel in Switzerland, for sizzle and fun.

Art Basel had another energizing effect: it shook up the torpid Miami museum scene, if indeed there really had been one before. Now, area museums have spruced up, expanded, brought in curators and directors of higher stature.

So, if you have any interest in real art, do some research and take some time to explore the many offerings.

MAINLAND ATTRACTIONS

BISCAYNE NATIONAL PARK

9700 SW 328th St., Homestead
305 230-7275
www.nps.gov/bisc
A 53-foot glass-bottom boat and a 45-foot diving and snorkeling catamaran takes you across southern Biscayne Bay, through wilderness, mangrove creeks, islands, and out to tropical coral reefs teeming with sea life. Family snorkeling and scuba diving available from the boat. Canoe and kayak rentals, picnic area, walking trails, fishing, camping and shower facilities available. Reservations

BISCAYNE NATURE CENTER

required. Waterfront visitor center offers exhibits, films and information. Open daily 8 a.m.-5:30p.m. Visitor Center open daily 8:30 a.m.-5 p.m. Glass-bottom boat tour: adults $24.45, children (12 and under) $16.45, seniors (62 and over) $19.45. Scuba diving $54, snorkeling: adults $35, children (12 and under) $29.95. Glass-bottom boat departs at 10 a.m., scuba/ family snorkel departs at 1:30 p.m. Scuba diving departs at 8:30 a.m.

BISCAYNE NATURE CENTER

Marjory Stoneman Douglas Biscayne Nature Center
6767 Crandon Blvd., Key Biscayne
305 361-6767, ext. 119
www.biscaynenaturecenter.org

Offers hands-on marine exploration, coastal hammock hikes, fossil-rock reef walks, local history lectures and beach walks. Marine exploration trips scheduled at low tide only. All trips led by naturalist guide. Reservations required. Call for tour information and reservations.

COOPERTOWN AIRBOAT RIDES

22700 SW 8th St., Miami
305 226-6048
www.coopertownairboats.com

Offering airboat rides and alligator exhibitions since 1945. Professional guides lead tours through Hardwood Hammock to see wildlife in its native Everglades environment. Just 11 miles west of Florida' s Turnpike. Gift shop and restaurant with a menu that includes frog legs and gator tail. Call ahead to book a private tour. Open daily 8 a.m.-7 p.m.

CORAL CASTLE MUSEUM

28655 S. Dixie Highway, Homestead-305-248-6345
www.coralcastle.com

This quirky monument is one of Greater Miami's more unusual attractions. Giant pieces of coral rock were carved into a variety of objects by Edward Leedskalnin in the 1920s, as a tribute to unrequited love. The construction techniques behind this mystery garden of fantastic coral sculptures continue to baffle experts and visitors. This attraction has been featured in hundreds of newspaper and magazine articles.

CORAL GABLES MERRICK HOUSE

907 Coral Way, Coral Gables
305 460-5391
www.coralgables.com

This is the boyhood home of George E. Merrick, founder and developer of the City of Coral Gables. This historic landmark originally began as an 1899 frame house, and was added onto in 1907. The house has been restored to the 1920s period and filled with the Merrick family's art, furniture and personal treasures. The park is open to the public on Wednesdays and Sundays for guided tours at 1, 2 and 3 p.m. Suggested admission, which includes the guided tour, is $5 for adults, $3 for seniors/students/ group tours, $1 for children ages 6-12, and free for children under 5 years old.

DOLPHIN HARBOR
Miami Seaquarium

4400 Rickenbacker Causeway , Miami-305-361-5705
www.miamiseaquarium.com

This new facility allows visitors to slip into a wet suit and for an up-close adventure with dolphins. With two different programs there is something for everyone. For the ride of a lifetime, enjoy the Dolphin Odyssey, a deep-water experience including a dorsal tow on one of the dolphins. Or book a Dolphin Encounter, a shallow-water experience where guests touch, feed and play with the dolphins. Looking for more of a behind the scenes experience, enroll to be Trainer for a Day. In this day-long program, guests experience how the facility keeps these marine mammals healthy and happy, plus enjoy a Dolphin Odyssey and get up close with the sea lions.

DRAGONFLY EXPEDITIONS

1825 Ponce de Leon Blvd., Suite 369, Coral Gables-305 774-9019
www.dragonflyexpeditions.com

These purveyors of uncommon adventures provide award-winning, distinctive group day and half-day journeys through the Everglades and Miami's colorful history for the sophisticated traveler.

EVERGLADES ALLIGATOR FARM

40351 SW 192nd Ave., Florida City
305-247-2628
www.everglades.com

Explore the Everglades on a thrilling airboat tour and enjoy live shows every hour featuring alligators and snakes. Open daily 9 a.m.-6 p.m. Adults $23 for farm, airboat ride and shows; children $15.50 for farm, airboat ride and shows; Adults farm admission only $15.50; children farm admission only $10.50.

EVERGLADES NATIONAL PARK

305-242-7799
www.nps.gov/ever/

There are several ways to get into the Everglades, so we strongly recommend you look over their web site to decide which way you want to experience this place. There's nothing else in the world like Everglades National Park, the largest subtropical wilderness in the United States, boasting rare and endangered species. It has been designated a World Heritage Site, International Biosphere Reserve, and Wetland of International Importance, significant to all people of the world. The fact that Big Sugar continues to pollute it and kill off hundreds of species with the collusion of both the Federal and State governments is another story, so we strongly urge you to see what's left of it while you can! It really ought to be seen in

DOLPHIN HARBOR

the summer, when it's rainy season, but then it's also most uncomfortable (those pesky mosquitoes). In the dry winter, the place is rather parched, so it doesn't have the same effect on you.

EVERGLADES SAFARI PARK
26700 Tamiami Trail
(SW 8th Street), Miami
305 226-6923
www.evergladessafaripark.com
The park features an alligator farm and show, guided airboat rides, a jungle trail, an interpretive center, a restaurant and a gift shop. Private tours are available. Open daily 8:30 a.m.-5 p.m. Adults $20, children (5-11) $10, children (under 5) free.

FAIRCHILD TROPICAL BOTANIC GARDEN
10901 Old Cutler Road, Coral Gables
305 667-1651
www.fairchildgarden.org
This premier conservation and education-based garden and recognized international leader in conservation is dedicated to exploring, explaining and conserving the world of tropical plants. It houses the National Palm Collection, has the world's greatest living collection of palms and cycads; an education program reaching more than 30,000 school children per year; hosts popular events like the International Mango and Orchid Festivals, the Ramble, concerts, affiliated plant society shows and sales; and is a not-for-profit organization relying on the support of its 40,000 members and benefactors. It hosts major events such as Les Lalanne at Fairchild in 2010 and 2011.

FROST MUSEUM OF SCIENCE
1101 Biscayne Blvd, Miami
305-434-9600
www.frostscience.org
ADMISSION: Nominal fee
NEIGBORHOOD: Downtown
A science museum, planetarium, and aquarium located in Museum Park in

downtown Miami tht opened in 2017. The museum is divided into four buildings: Frost Planetarium, Aquarium, and North and West Wings. The three-level aquarium may be the star attraction of this venue but it's also a learning and hands-on museum with lots of interactive exhibits. Learn the core science behind living systems, the solar system and known universe, the physics of flight, light and lasers, the biology of the human body and mind, and more. The 250,000 square foot museum sits on four acres within the waterfront Museum Park across from PAMM (Perez Art Museum Miami).

FRUIT & SPICE PARK

24801 SW 187th Ave., Homestead
305-247-5727
www.redlandfruitandspice.com /
Established in 1944, this tropical paradise is nestled in the heart of the Redland District, just 35 miles south of Downtown Miami. More than 500 varieties of exotic fruits, herbs, spices and nuts from throughout the world are found in this lush 39-acre park. Open daily except Christmas Day 9 a.m.-5 p.m. Guided tours conducted daily on a tour tram at 11, 1:30 and 3, and are included in the price of admission. Adults $6, children (6-12) $1.50, under 6 free. Gift shop on site. Picnic facilities available.

GLOBAL AIR GROUP

603 SW 77th Way, Pembroke Pines
954-605-8155 / 954-639-4010
www.tourhelicopter.com
This one is centrally located in downtown Miami – you actually have to take a short boat ride from their dock in Bayside Marina to their floating helipad in the Bay. Close to South Beach.

GO MIAMI CARD

Miami Beach Visitor Center
Miami Beach Convention Center -
800-887-9103
http://www.gomiamicard.com
Miami's multi-attraction pass featuring more than 40 Miami area attractions plus discounts on shopping and dining. Customers may choose from one, two, three, five or seven days of unlimited admission to Miami's very best attractions, museums, tours and cruises, and have two weeks to use it. The card gives visitors the ultimate tailor-made destination experience at a great value. Attractions include Miami Seaquarium, Jungle Island, Duck Tours and many more.

GRAY LINE MIAMI

Miami: 877-643-1258
www.graylinemiami.com
This company has 100 years of tradition and history and operates in 150 destinations around the world. Offering travelers and their representatives the full range of inbound/receptive tour operator services: sightseeing tours, private charter transportation that gives individual and group travelers the opportunity to stay and enjoy the many amazing and unique features that South Florida has to offer. Now operating Gray Line signature Miami Sightseeing Hop On-Hop Off.

HAULOVER BEACH PARK / NUDE BEACH

10800 Collins Ave., Bal Harbour
305-947-3525 /
www.miamidade.gov/parks/parks/haulover_park.asp
Has one of the most beautiful beaches – a mile and a half stretch. Open ocean surf, various shaded picnic facilities, beautifully landscaped sand dunes, and

concession stands. The beach is ideal for surfing as well as swimming. Guarded by well-trained lifeguards. Across the street from the beach, Haulover Park has a full-service marina, restaurant, tennis courts, family 9-hole golf course, sundries shop and kite shops. The northern portion of this beach is for nudists.

HELICOPTER TOURS

There's more than one service: click below to go to individual listings in this chapter:

Global Air

Miami Executive Helicopters

HISTORICAL MUSEUM OF SOUTHERN FLORIDA

101 W. Flagler St., Miami
305-375-1492
www.hmsf.org

Although this beautiful facility is tucked in the middle of what constitutes "downtown Miami," it's still worth a trek, even though it's a pain in the ass to get to if you're a tourist, requiring a bus or a $20-$25 cab ride. The Historical Museum of Southern Florida tells the stories of South Florida and the Caribbean. It's one of the largest private, regional history museums in the country.

ISLAND QUEEN CRUISES

Bayside Marketplace, 401 Biscayne Blvd., Miami, 305 379-5119
www.islandqueencruises.com

Sit back and relax for an unforgettable bilingual narrated sightseeing cruise along scenic Biscayne Bay. See Miami's spectacular coastal sites including the beautiful Downtown Miami skyline, the Port of Miami, Fisher Island, Miami Beach and "Millionaire's Row" - the homes of the rich and famous. Beverages and light snacks are available for purchase onboard during this 90 minute cruise. All of their modern yachts feature an air-conditioned lower salon, enclosed in picture windows, as well as an upper-deck where guests may take in the fresh ocean breeze under a protective awning. Please arrive at their ticket booth 30 minutes prior to departure to receive boarding passes. Departs every hour on the hour from 11 a.m. to 7 p.m., every day.

KITEBOARDING

6767 Crandon Blvd., Key Biscayne
305-345-9974
www.miamikiteboarding.com

You actually have to learn how to fly a kite before you become a kiteboarder. You will need several hours of lessons.

MIAMI CULINARY TOURS

1000 5th St., Suite 200, Miami Beach:
786-942-8856
www.miamiculinarytours.com

This company offers the South Beach Food Tour and the Little Havana Food Tour. Both tours provide a non-touristy, local experience so attendees get the opportunity to immerse themselves into the local culture, and feel and eat like a native. The tours blend a historical, architectural and cultural experience together with an intimate, behind-the-scenes culinary introduction to savor the best cuisine the area has to offer - all at an affordable price.

MIAMI EXECUTIVE HELICOPTERS

Tamiami Airport
14150 SW 129 St., 786-507-5200
www.miamiheli.com

Take friends and family on a one-of-a-kind helicopter adventure over Miami. The helicopter travels just a few hundred feet off the ground over the coastline of Key Biscayne, Viscaya Museum & Gardens, Brickell, Downtown Miami, Bayside,

KITTEBOARDING

American Airlines Arena, the major cruise ships in the Port of Miami, and Miami Beach, where some of South Florida's most famous residents live. This helicopter tour is equipped with a headset for every passenger and air conditioning. The Pilot provides play-by-play experience. FAA Certified.

ZOO MIAMI

12400 SW 152nd St., Miami
305 251-0400
www.zoomiami.org/

A wonderful place, but sadly in the middle of Nowhere. It's only convenient if you're on your way to Key West or the Federal Prison located right next door. (This is where they kept Noriega.) Best to just plan a day trip here, because it'll take half the day to get there and back, depending on traffic. Their web site has all the pertinent information. Rated one of the top 10 zoos in the U.S. by Tripadvisor.com in 2008, this 340-acre zoo showcases more than 2,000 animals including koalas, flamingos and elephants in large open-air exhibits. Things to do and see include: the 27-acre Amazon and Beyond, American Banker's Family Aviary, Dr. Wilde's World, Samburu Giraffe Feeding Station, Humpy's Camel Rides, Nick Jr.'s favorite animal rescuer Diego, and zookeeper talks throughout the day. Rent a Safari Cycle, ride the monorail or take a guided tram tour to see the zoo. Picnic and party facilities are available. Open daily 9:30 a.m.-5:30 p.m. (ticket booths close at 4 p.m.). Admission: Adults (age 13 & up) $15.95, children (ages 3-12) $11.95, plus tax. Visit their website for an online admission coupon at the bottom of the Visit the Zoo page.

MIAMI NICE TOURS

305 949-9180
www.miami-nice.com

This company offers tours, packages, hotels, transfers and charters. Comprehensive city tours are offered in English, German, French, Italian and Spanish. They also provide airport transfers and charters on luxury buses.

ZOO MIAMI

They have provided great service since 1987, and all major Internet travel sites work with them. See the best of Florida during one of their daily tours to the Everglades, Key West and Orlando. No group is too big or too small. The company also offers great deals on three- to five-star hotel specials included with a tour and transportation.

MIAMI SEAPLANE TOURS

3401 Rickenbacker Causeway, Key Biscayne-305 361-3909
www.miamiseaplane.com

Experience the thrill and romance of skipping across the wave tops as the seaplane becomes airborne, unveiling the magical city skyline beneath. Choose seaplane tours from 30 minutes to two hours. Reservation required with 24 hours notice.

MIAMI SEAQUARIUM

4400 Rickenbacker Causeway, Virginia Key: 305-361-5705
www.miamiseaquarium.com

Located on the causeway road to Key Biscayne. A 38-acre tropical paradise with spectacular skyline views of downtown Miami, this is the center of the action if you want to swim with the dolphins, or as they now call it, "dolphin interaction." The dolphins walk on water and killer whales fly through the air. Sea lions delight children of all ages and endangered sea turtles and manatees live here. Enjoy a world-class marine-life entertainment park with eight different marine animal shows and astonishing daily presentations.

MONKEY JUNGLE

14805 SW 216 St., South Miami
305-235-1611
www.monkeyjungle.com

When Joseph DuMond, an inquisitive animal behaviorist, released six monkeys into the wilds of a dense South Florida hammock in 1933, he didn't realize his endeavors would help shape the attitudes of many in the primatological and zoological fields. The release fifty years ago of that small Java troop signified the beginning of the larger thriving troop that runs free here at Monkey Jungle today.

JUNGLE ISLAND

Watson Island
305-400-7000
www.jungleisland.com
On the island in Biscayne Bay between Miami and South Beach along the MacArthur Causeway. Birds, mammals, primates, fish.

SCHNEBLY REDLAND'S WINERY

30205 SW 217th Ave., Homestead
305-242-1224
www.schneblywinery.com
This winery in the Redland tropical countryside offers tours and wine tastings around natural coral waterfalls surrounded by lush tropical foliage. Visitors can compare the taste of lychee, passion fruit, carambola, guava and mango wines, just to name a few. This is the southernmost winery in the Continental U.S., handcrafting tropical wines without using grapes. The Grand Tasting Room has a Southern plantation agricultural style. The building is 5,000 square feet and has a view of the tropical courtyard, waterfalls, winery and Grand Tiki, Waterfall Tiki and more than 20,000 square feet of connecting Tikis. They host weddings and corporate retreats. Buses are welcome.

TRAVEL TRACKERS INC.

305 205-0219
www.traveltrackers.com
This full-service USA travel, convention, event and meeting receptive company provides the tri-county area with concierge services and custom tours of Miami, the Everglades, Orlando and the Florida Keys for corporate groups and individuals. They arrange private transportation with bilingual meet-and-greet services at airports, seaports and hotels. A website brochure is available online or mailed on request.

VENETIAN POOL

2701 De Soto Blvd., Coral Gables
305-460-5306
www.gablesrecreation.com
A Venetian-style lagoon carved out of coral rock, this historic landmark and swimming pool features caves, stone bridges and waterfalls. Operates year-round. Call for information on rates and hours of operation. Children must be 38 inches tall or show proof that they are 3 years old. Open 7 days a week from Memorial Day through Labor Day, closed Mondays during the rest of the year.

VIZCAYA MUSEUM & GARDENS

3251 S. Miami Ave., Miami
305-250-9133
www.vizcaya.org
Built by agricultural industrialist James Deering in 1916, Vizcaya Museum & Gardens features a main house, ten acres of formal gardens, a hardwood hammock, and soon-to-be-restored historic village. (We think this is one of the best things to do in the whole County.)

YACHT BRASIL MOTORBOATS & CHARTERS

300 Alton Rd., Suite 108, Miami Beach:
305-722-7200
www.yachtbrasilusa.com
This company offers a fleet of vessels for cruising pleasure in Miami and around South Florida. They offer half-day charters, full-day charters, as well as term (week or longer) charters. They can also accommodate groups up to 400 passengers on larger vessels they work with.

Chapter 6
SHOPPING & SERVICES

Miami has some excellent shopping opportunities. For high-end shopping, you have Bal Harbour where all the brands you'd find in London, Paris or New York have impressive satellite shops. Then there's everywhere else…

This section is divided into 3 parts: **Bal Harbour**; **South Beach** (with breakdown listings for Ocean Drive, Washington & Collins, Lincoln Road, Espanola Way; and **Mainland Shopping** (with short descriptions of the major shopping areas).

BAL HARBOUR

Most **serious** shoppers make the fifteen-minute drive north of South Beach to 96th Street on Collins Avenue where they can feel enormous comfort perusing the extensive (and expensive) wares at the Miami outposts of such notable names as Cartier, Bulgari, Harry Winston, Armani, Brioni, Bruno Cicinelli, Chanel, Coco Paris, Dior, D&G, Pucci, Ferragamo, Graff, Hermes, Jimmy Choo, Lacoste, Ralph Lauren, Tiffany and even tired old Brooks Brothers.

Anchored by Saks and Neiman's, Bal Harbour Shops is still the place to go. Thankfully, it's concealed from the hoi polloi by tall thick walls. They even charge you for parking, which helps to keep the riff-raff out. (These people were the first ever to charge for parking in a mall.)

But, even if you're not in the mood to buy, it's still fun to stroll through the meticulously landscaped open-air tropical courtyard the Whitman family has created for your enjoyment while you shop. The grounds are rigorously maintained. Flawlessly. It's just a splendid way to spend the afternoon. My niece Sophie lives just behind Neiman's in Bal Harbour Village. There's a little locked gate she can slip through to meet me for luncheon at in the Bal Harbour shops when I make the trek north. (The steak tartare is not as good as Joe Allen's used to be, believe it or not, but the French fries are skinny, crisp, piping hot and delish. Add a bottle of

BAL HARBOUR

Sancerre or Brouilly and what more could one want?)

The fountains here are loud, lush and wonderful. Nowhere else in Miami will you find fountains gushing, rushing and slushing so dramatically. If water is money, they throw it away for your pleasure here in Bal Harbour. I look at those sad little fountains on Lincoln Road and think of one word: **pathetic**. To hear the tiny little sprinkling sounds they make reminds you some bum peeing in an alley. (If you don't believe me, go into one of the alleys on South Beach at three in the morning and you can hear this sound for yourself.) Open Monday-Saturday 10 a.m.-9 p.m., Sunday noon-6 p.m.

SOUTH BEACH

OCEAN DRIVE
WASHINGTON & COLLINS
LINCOLN ROAD
ESPANOLA WAY

OCEAN DRIVE

You can totally forget touristy Ocean Drive (in terms of shopping). But for a certain kind of tourist, Ocean Drive is a favorite, and hanging out at one of the bumper-to-bumper cafés on South Beach's most famous street sipping gigantic cocktails while watching the parade of people is mandatory. **Mango's** is one spot that is either the apogee (or the nadir, depending on your view) of what it means to be on Ocean Drive. All the servers perform. The **Clevelander** is like a college frat party on Spring Break where no one ever went back to school. But shopping, no. Just the usual touristy stuff you'd expect.

WASHINGTON & COLLINS

The other main street on South Beach is Washington Avenue, which runs parallel to Collins Avenue. I'm convinced whatever poor people are left on South Beach (and there are more than you think) do nothing all day but walk up and down Washington Avenue, making it look worse than it already is. Washington Avenue may be the slummiest street on South Beach, but there's no mistaking its funky allure.

Art Deco fans should take note of the **Art Deco Post Office** and the **Wolfsonian Museum** (filled with lots of examples of Art Deco, it also has a wonderful café and bookstore). The **World Erotic Art Museum** (an amazing collection of erotic art from around the globe) is a must-see for fans of erotica and the unusual.

My "best finds" on these two streets:

DIESEL

933 Lincoln Rd., Miami Beach
786-718-1555 www.diesel.com

Strictly European in its designs, this store offers a variety of designer jeans, shirts, and accessories.

HELIUM

760 Ocean Dr., Miami Beach
305-538-4111

Drop in at this charming little classy gift shop tucked away around the corner.

ARMANI EXCHANGE

760 Collins Ave., Miami Beach
305-531-5900
www.armaniexchange.com

Here you'll find Armani's more affordable line including jeans, t-shirts and watches.

CLUB MONACO

624 Collins Ave., Miami Beach
305-674-7446 www.clubmonaco.com

The hottest designer looks for men and women, right out of the latest fashion mags, at affordable prices.

GIROUX

638 Collins Ave., Miami Beach
305-672-3015

This is the hottest shoe store in town, featuring their own designs (shoes, handbags, belts), but also with names like Michael Kors.

THE WEBSTER

1220 Collins Ave., Miami Beach
305-674-7899
www.thewebstermiami.com

The Webster is a 20,000 square feet high luxury multi-brand fashion store. It is located in the heart of Miami Beach in a historic Art Deco building designed in 1939 by famed architect Henry Hohauser. The three-level store is devoted to fashion (men's and women's ready-to-wear and luxury accessories such as shoes, bags, jewelry and watches), photography and entertainment. It's crammed with vintage watches from Rolex, Patek Philippe, Breitling, Cartier, and Longines, and clothing from Marc Jacobs, Givenchy, Tom Ford, Lanvin, Neil Barrett, Trussardi 1911, and Adam Kimmel, plus lots more.

MAC COSMETICS

673A Collins Ave., 305-604-9040
1107 Lincoln Road, 305-538-1088
www.maccosmetics.com

This shop is the center of the universe for MAC lovers featuring every color you can imagine for eyes, cheeks and lips, from electric blue mascara to deep purple lipstick.

LINCOLN ROAD MALL

URBAN OUTFITTERS

841 Lincoln Rd.,Miami Beach
305-534-5166
www.urbanoutfitters.com

Direct from NYC with a South Beach twist, here you'll find two floors of the funkiest and trendiest fashions as well as some of the coolest toys, books, and accessories for your apartment (shag rugs, lamps, mobiles, and even shower curtains).

LINCOLN ROAD SHOPPING DISTRICT

Collins Avenue to Bay Road,
between 16th and 17th streets
(& the Bay to the ocean), Miami Beach
305 672-1270
http://www.shoponmiamibeach.com

Lincoln Road is a pedestrian mall that traverses the island east to west from the ocean to the Bay. It is a shopping, dining and cultural center featuring unique shops, galleries and restaurants with indoor and outdoor seating—perfect for people watching.

Unfortunately, a lot of chains have encroached on Lincoln Road as national brands with deep pockets install stores here for "branding" purposes and landlords hike the rents. So now there's a GAP, a Victoria's Secret, a Pottery Barn, crap like that. All this homogenizes the Road, giving it less character. But there are some good spots. Take a walk and discover them.

Lincoln Road is a people-watchers' dream and shopper's paradise, filled with sidewalk cafes and an amazing variety of boutiques. Much to the consternation of a lot of locals, national brands have bought their way onto Lincoln Road, displacing one-of-a-kind shops as the rents soared skyward. So you find name stores like **Gap, Victoria's Secret, Bebe, French Connection, Guess, Swatch, Diesel** and **Steve Madden**. But even if you're not shopping, you can enjoy a heady view of Art Deco architecture.

7 FOR ALL MANKIND

1008 Lincoln Rd., Miami Beach
305-538-7355 www.7forallmankind.com
Born in L.A. in the fall of 2000, this store changed the landscape of premium denim offerings. You can get "selvage" denim here, a term derived from "self-edge," which refers to uncut edges that occur when shuttle looms weave a continuous thread down the length of the fabric. Men, women and kids, in all styles.

ALCHEMIST

1109 Lincoln Rd., Miami Beach
305-531-4653
1111 Lincoln Rd., carpark Level 5, Miami Beach: 305-531-4815
www.shopalchemist.com
The striking design of this store is by Rene Gonzalez. The layered white squared-off arches with recessed lighting are visually stunning. Givenchy dresses, other haute labels like Rick Owens, Martin Margiela. You've got to visit the store on the fifth floor of the Herzog & de Meuron parking garage at 111l Lincoln Road. Go up for the view and have a look at their high-end duds. This place is refreshingly European and a welcome respite from all the crappy tourist traps on South Beach.

ALLSAINTS

910 Lincoln Rd., Miami Beach
786-517-8181
www.us.allsaints.com
Wide array of apparel for men and women: coats, leather, sweaters, boots and shoes, accessories, bags. The jeans here can be edgy, part retro hippie, part rock n roll. Jeans with metallic highlights are popular, with rises ranging from low-waist to drop-crotch. Polos, sweatshirts, T-shirts.

BRITTO CENTRAL

818 & 1102 Lincoln Rd.
305-531-8821
www.britto.com
Gallery of local artist **Romero Britto** which includes exhibitions of his colorful art plus a gift shop (for those who can't afford the real art) that includes calendars, mugs, watches, posters and more.

BOOKS & BOOKS

927 Lincoln Rd., Miami Beach
305-532-3222
www.booksandbooks.com
Books & Books Shop & Café are located in the historic Art Deco Sterling Building and is worth a visit whether you're a book lover or not. The store specializes in art, design, fashion and architecture. This is the South Beach branch of the famous bookstore headquartered in Coral Gables. It's just down the short breezeway—ask any of the waiters at the café in front and they will direct you.

DECO DRIVE CIGARS

1436 Ocean Dr., 305-672-9032
1650 Meridian Ave., 305-674-1811
414 Lincoln Rd., 305-531-8388
www.decodrivecigars.com
Hey, you can't come to Miami without buying cigars to take home. Here's the best place on South Beach offering the finest selection of cigars and smoking accessories.

THE DOG BAR

1684 Jefferson Ave., Miami Beach
305-532-5654
www.dogbar.com
Pet lovers flock to this unique full service luxury specialty pet supply store that features the latest in dog and cat merchandise. (Just off Lincoln Road.)

ESPAÑOLA WAY

DYLAN'S CANDY BAR
801 Lincoln Rd., Miami Beach
305-531-1988
www.dylanscandybar.com
Ralph Lauren's daughter has carved out a special niche for herself in retail, and it has nothing to do with clothing. She's the Candy Queen of New York, and now has a shop on the very expensive corner of Meridian and Lincoln. Cocktails are served outside on Lincoln Road, but not with booze: a chocolate daiquiri, anyone? They don't just sell some of the world's best candy here; they "curate" it, according to Dylan. Interesting novelty items and some accessories as well.

STEVE MADDEN
443 Lincoln Rd., Miami Beach
305-673-9997
www.stevemadden.com.
Shoes, shoes and more shoes. (Interesting accessories, too.)

ESPANOLA WAY
While the city and other guidebooks call this street a "Spanish village," or a "Mediterranean village," and always call it "quaint" and "charming," it's really just a couple of blocks off Washington Avenue (between Fourteenth and Fifteenth streets). On the east end, the Washington Avenue end, there's a youth hostel and a few tourist-trap eateries, so it's always a bustling corner. There are several really good restaurants here now. (See chapter on Restaurants.) On the west end you'll find a little creperie, **A La Folie**, that's quite nice, where you can sit out under a few shady trees. I've found a few interesting spots for you to visit, though:

MAINLAND SHOPPING

BRICKELL CITY CENTRE

701 S Miami Ave
Miami Fl 33131
www.brickellcitycentre.com
Four levels of luxury, premium and world-class dining and entertainment are interconnected over three city blocks and anchored by a 107,000 square foot Saks Fifth Avenue and luxury VIP Cinema Experience from CMX.

COCOWALK

3015 Grand Ave., Coconut Grove
305 444-0777
www.cocowalk.net
This retail center is situated in one of Miami's oldest and most prominent communities. Its opening is probably the single most important thing that killed the Grove as a desirable place to be.This ghastly place is cluttered with mid to low-level crap like the GAP, Victoria's Secret, FYE Music Store, Maui Nix Surf, Starbucks. In June 2010 it welcomed the Paragon Grove 13 luxury movie theatre. According to their PR department: "Nightly live music and special events are always taking place in this exciting retail and entertainment center."Well, I'm not so sure about "exciting."

DADELAND MALL

US 1 & State Road 826 (formal address is 7535 N. Kendall Dr.), Kendall
305-665-6226
www.simon.com/mall/dadeland-mall
Huge suburban mall with a wide variety of shopping options: Macy's (the biggest one in Florida), JCPenney, Nordstrom's and Saks Fifth Avenue. Specialty stores include Abercrombie & Fitch, Ann Taylor, Apple, Banana Republic, Coach, The Disney Store, Guess, L'Occitane, Sephora, Talbots, Vertigo, and Victoria's Secret, the country's largest The Limited and Express; more than 185 specialty stores including Abercrombie & Fitch, Apple, J. Crew, bebe, White House I Black Market, Zara, A/X Exchange, Movado, Lucky Brand Jeans, Swarovski, True Religion Brand Jeans and numerous eateries like The Cheesecake Factory and Johnny Rockets.

MIAMI DESIGN DISTRICT

NE 36th to 42nd streets (between NE 2nd Ave. and N Miami Ave.), Miami, 305-772-7100
www.miamidesigndistrict.net
This is one of Miami's most exciting neighborhoods for design, art and other creative companies. It is right in the heart of the city, just 10 minutes from Downtown Miami and directly across the Causeway from Miami Beach (Tuttle Causeway at 41st Street).

Store and showroom listings, events and more are available online or over the phone. Great new places for lunch when you want a break. This area made history in the shopping world in 2012 when Louis Vuitton left the Bal Harbour Shops (horrors!) and decamped to the Design District. Other big names (Gucci, Cartier) have followed and other are expected to come here as well as leases come up for renewal in Bal Harbour. Construction is currently underway to create a pedestrian friendly street that will mimic Bal Harbour's famous open-air oasis.

DOWNTOWN MIAMI SHOPPING DISTRICT
Biscayne Boulevard to 2nd Avenue West; SE 1st Street to NE 3rd Street, Miami: 305-379-7070
http://www.downtownmiami.com
Historic Flagler Street is the heart of the City of Miami. Hundreds of stores and shops make up the Downtown Shopping District, anchored by Macy's, Marshalls, Ross Dress for Less, and La Epoca (imported from Havana). Visitors can shop all day, lunch on food from almost anywhere in the world, visit art and historical museums, or just stroll the streets of Miami's historic district. Also the destination for world-class jewelry shopping, including the Seybold Building which boasts more than 280 jewelers. Take the Downtown Miami Partnership historic walking tour every Saturday at 10:30 a.m. Call for reservations.

BAYSIDE MARKETPLACE
401 Biscayne Blvd., Miami
305-577-3344
www.baysidemarketplace.com
A dining, entertainment and retail complex located on beautiful Biscayne Bay in Downtown Miami. Visitors will find more than 150 shops, restaurants and bars, including national retailers and unique shops, Miami's Hard Rock Cafe, Bubba Gump Shrimp Co., and an "international" food court that's really scary.
Free nightly entertainment at the waterfront Marina stage.
Tour boats offer sightseeing or dance cruises throughout the day. Ideal for group outings and special events.
Hours of operation for this outdoor festival center are Monday-Thursday retail 10 a.m.-10 p.m.; Friday & Saturday 10 a.m.-11 p.m.; Sunday 11 a.m.-9 p.m. Restaurants and bars stay open later. Live music until 11 p.m. Sunday-Thursday, and until 12:30 a.m. Friday and Saturday.

THE FALLS
US 1 & SW 136th St., South Miami
305-255-4571
www.simon.com/mall/the-falls
Has a great mix of great shopping and restaurants in a nice outdoor setting. Open-air mall has top department and specialty stores Bloomingdale's, Hollister, Brooks Brothers, Macy's, Crate & Barrel, many more.

MARY BRICKELL VILLAGE
901 S. Miami Ave., Miami
305-381-6130
www.marybrickellvillage.com
This retail and restaurant destination is right in the center of everything. Tenants include Balans Restaurant, Rosa Mexicano, P.F. Chang's, Oceanaire Room, Starbucks and Regions Bank.

MIAMI INTERNATIONAL MALL

1455 NW 107th Ave., Doral
305-593-1777
http://www.simon.com

West of town, almost in the Everglades, you'll find this mall with 5 department stores: Macy's - Men's and Home; Women's & Children's, JCPenney, Sears and Kohl's. More than 140 specialty stores including Ann Taylor Loft, Bebe, Best Buy Mobile, Cache, Coach, Express/ Express Men, Forever 21, Gap, Guess, Gymboree, Hollister, Mayor's Jewelers, Nine West, Old Navy, Disney Store, The Limited, Tous, Victoria's Secret and White House/Black Market. A children's play area and a postal store are located in the mall for added convenience, as well as 22 eateries including an Argentine steakhouse, The Knife.

AVENTURA MALL

19501 Biscayne Blvd., Aventura
305-935-1110
http://www.aventuramall.com

A premier shopping and dining destination, this 2.7 million-square-foot mall boasts 300 stores and restaurants including The Grill on the Alley and Grand Lux Café, and Turnberry for the Arts, featuring works by renowned international and South Florida artists. It is home to Nordstrom, Bloomingdale's, Macy's and an array of internationally recognized brands, including Burberry, Façonnable, Calvin Klein, Anthropologie, M Missoni, BCBGMaxAzria, Apple, Abercrombie & Fitch, A/X Armani Exchange, Herve Leger by Max Azria, Diesel, Juicy Couture, Gap, Kenneth Cole, Tourneau, Henri Bendel, Urban Outfitters, 7 for all Mankind and Sony Style.

DOWNTOWN CORAL GABLES/ MIRACLE MILE

220 Miracle Mile, Coral Gables
305-569-0311
http://www.shopcoralgables.com

When I was a kid, my grandmother used to drag me down here to go with her as she shopped "The Mile." Still features quality shops, art galleries, boutiques, restaurants and a live theater (Actors Playhouse, does top quality work) in a lushly landscaped environment of tree-lined streets. Shoppers will find unique jewelry, apparel, home furnishings, salons and spas, and other specialty shops.

VILLAGE OF MERRICK PARK

358 San Lorenzo Ave., Coral Gables
305-529-1215
www.villageofmerrickpark.com

A lot of great names down here: Aldolfo Dominguez, Ann Taylor, Jimmy Choo, Lacoste, Benetton, Mayors, Betsey Johnson, Neiman Marcus, Cache, C'est Bon, Coach, Cole Haan, a hundred more. Easy to spend a day here.

HISTORIC DOWNTOWN HOMESTEAD

41 N. Krome Ave., Homestead
305-323-6564
www.cityofhomestead.com

Historic Downtown Homestead features art galleries, antique shops and specialty restaurants, but the real reason to come down her is to get good (and authentic) Mexican food cheap. (The Mexicans pick all the tomatoes.)

Chapter 7
SPAS

BILTMORE SPA
1200 Anastasia Ave., Coral Gables
305-913-3187
http://www.biltmorespa.com
Located on the seventh floor, with panoramic views from floor to ceiling windows, this spa's elite facilities are impressive. Beige and green earth tones, natural woods and the quiet murmur of falling water enhance an environment of calm and beauty. The spa offers a wide selection of therapies and treatments customized to help guests achieve long-term benefits and individualized wellness. Their menu includes a selection of massage therapies, skin care services, body treatments and wraps, signature couples' treatments, and a full-service hair and nail salon.

BLISS SPA
W SOUTH BEACH HOTEL
2201 Collins Ave., Miami Beach
305-938-3123
http://www.blissworld.com
This spa combines a clever menu of super-effective spa services with a fun, "no-attitude" atmosphere. Guests can expect 7,300 square feet of tension-fighting facilities, a retail beauty boutique featuring the best in beauty, a nail lounge with two manicure and two pedicure stations, and luxe men's and women's lounges. Trademark Bliss touches — like rhythm and blues tunes and the legendary brownie buffet — set a fun, upbeat tone to top off the space.

GUYAND GIRL SALON & SPA
Mondrian, 1100 West Ave., Miami Beach: 305-514-1950
www.mondrian-miami.com
This spa features 4,000 square feet of Marcel Wanders-designed interiors with six treatment rooms equipped to offer an extensive variety of services. Along with signature Milk and Honey treatments and private garden-view terrace, the spa is an exclusive carrier of products by SJAL and Butter London.

LAPIS SPA
FONTAINEBLEAU MIAMI BEACH

4441 Collins Ave., Miami Beach
305-674-4772
www.fontainebleau.com

This two-level spa harnesses the natural qualities of water to create a shared experience that is both restorative and renewing. Mineral rich water in many forms is used throughout the 40,000-square-foot spa that features 30 private treatment rooms as well as a co-ed pool and lounge area. Merging age-old techniques with the latest contemporary technology and design, this spa provides guests with stress relief, anti-aging and wellness solutions.

RITZ-CARLTON SPA,
KEY BISCAYNE

455 Grand Bay Dr., Key Biscayne
305-365-4157
www.ritzcarlton.com

An oasis of tropical splendor, this award-winning 20,000-square-foot retreat features a menu with ocean-inspired natural therapies, an exclusive Prada beauty line, a dedicated menu of services for gentlemen, 21 treatment rooms, a Wellness and Fitness center, relaxation lounges, a private pedicure suite, a Pilates studio and attentive staff to complete the spa experience.

STANDARD SPA MIAMI BEACH

40 Island Ave., Miami Beach
305-673-1717
http://www.standardhotel.com

This holistic and hydrotherapy-oriented spa hotel is inspired by global bathing cultures, self-teaching and healing. Located on the waters of Belle Isle, Miami Beach, this contemporary spa encourages the communal, shared rituals of ancient bathing traditions, with a Turkish-style Hamam, Roman waterfall, Aroma steam room, Finnish sauna and mud baths.

SPA V

1144 Ocean Dr., Miami Beach
305-728-6500
www.hotelvictorsouthbeach.com

This 6,000-square-foot oasis of rejuvenation and relaxation embraces ancient traditions of beauty and cleansing within a setting of modern luxury. The spa offers a full range of distinctive European-inspired treatments including Hammam V, the traditional Moroccan practice of cleansing the body with black olive beldi soap, then exfoliating with a Hammam glove, followed by a mask of Moroccan lava clay and hydrating massage. The Melt Me Massage is designed to melt away tension and stress from head to toe.

SPA AT GROVE ISLE

4 Grove Isle Dr., Miami
305-858-8300
http://www.groveisle.com

Rejuvenating mind, body and soul, this 6,000-square-foot spa guides enthusiasts on a sensory-seizing journey boasting one of five Watsu pools on the East Coast of the U.S. as well as Thai- and Indonesian-inspired rituals, private couples Zen steam room, relaxation room and outdoor Yoga deck. The spa combines water and relaxation, offering outdoor bayside massages as well as Watsu, or water shiatsu, massage, taking guests to yet another level of inner peace.

SPA AT SHORE CLUB

1901 Collins Ave., Miami Beach
305-695-3292
www.shoreclub.com

This beautiful rooftop retreat is an 8,000-square-foot full-service facility. It features a serene Zen-like atmosphere with teak and warm-toned materials, wet and dry treatment rooms, outdoor terraces and massage decks, and exclusive products. Guests can indulge in magnificent ocean views while rejuvenating their Yin Yang energies and replenishing their natural body rhythms. The spa offers an exclusive selection of massage, facial, body and nail treatments for women and men, available in private suites or outdoor terraces.

THE SPA AT ONE BAL HARBOUR

10295 Collins Ave., Bal Harbour
305-455-5400
http://www.oneluxuryhotels.com/spa.html

This spa offers five-star delivery of beauty and well-being treatments, including personalized facials, body sublimation, 5-senses hydrotherapy, harmonizing massage, intensive hand and foot therapies and totally transforming day experience packages.

Chapter 8
PARKING GARAGES

SOUTH BEACH - ALTON ROAD / WEST AVENUE / SUNSET HARBOUR - SOFI (SOUTH OF FIFTH) - LINCOLN ROAD - OCEAN / COLLINS / WASHINGTON / ESPANOLA - CAUSEWAYS FROM MIAMI

PARKING GARAGES
It's true. Parking is the ultimate nightmare on South Beach. Just be sure to park in a designated spot because you WILL BE TOWED. Two towing companies have a monopoly on South Beach towing. Both companies are represented by local power brokers and the city gets a kickback (uh, sorry, an "administrative fee") every time a car is towed. It ought to be a disgrace, but it's the way it is.

The absolute best way to enjoy South Beach if you are driving over in your own car or a rental is to park the car in a garage (like the one centrally located just north of Lincoln Road on 17th Street), leave it there and take **UBER.** This is what I do. I leave my car parked in front of my house, especially after 6 or 7 in the evening when it's hard to find a good space and then I take UBER all over town. You'll ride in nicer cars for cheaper fares and there's no tipping. If you don't have the Uber ap, download it now on your smartphone and use my code when you sign up and get $20 worth of free rides. Code is – **Andrewd145**

INDEX

Symbols

A

B

C

D

H

I

J

K

L

M

N

O

P

Q

R

S

T

U

V

W

X

Y

Z

Other Books by the Same Author

Andrew Delaplaine has written in widely varied fields: screenplays, novels (adult and juvenile), travel writing, journalism. His books are available in quality bookstores as well as all online retailers.

JACK HOUSTON / ST. CLAIR POLITICAL THRILLERS

THE KEYSTONE FILE – PART 1 - 7

On Election night, as China and Russia mass soldiers on their common border in preparation for war, there's a tie in the Electoral College that forces the decision for President into the House of Representatives as mandated by the Constitution. The incumbent Republican President, working through his Aide for Congressional Liaison, uses the Keystone File, which contains dirt on every member of Congress, to blackmail members into supporting the Republican candidate. The action runs from Election Night in November to Inauguration Day on January 20. Jack Houston St. Clair runs a small detective agency in Miami. His father is Florida Governor Sam Houston St. Clair, the Republican candidate. While he tries to help his dad win the election, Jack also gets hired to follow up on some

suspicious wire transfers involving drug smugglers, leading him to a sunken narco-sub off Key West that has $65 million in cash in its hull.

AFTER THE OATH: DAY ONE
AFTER THE OATH: MARCH WINDS
WEDDING AT THE WHITE HOUSE

Only three months have passed since Sam Houston St. Clair was sworn in as the new President, but a lot has happened. Returning from Vienna where he met with Russian and Chinese diplomats, Sam is making his way back to Flagler Hall in Miami, his first trip home since being inaugurated. Son Jack is in the midst of turmoil of his own back in Miami, dealing with various dramas, not the least of which is his increasing alienation from Babylon Fuentes and his growing attraction to the seductive Lupe Rodriguez. Fernando Pozo addresses new problems as he struggles to expand Cuba's secret operations in the U.S., made even more difficult as U.S.-Cuban relations thaw. As his father returns home, Jack knows Sam will find as much trouble at home as he did in Vienna.

THE ADVENTURES OF SHERLOCK HOLMES IV

In this series, the original Sherlock Holmes's great-great-great grandson solves crimes and mysteries in the present day, working out of the boutique whotel he owns on South Beach.

THE OKEECHOBEE MURDER

Sherlock Holmes and Watson are called to a remote area of Florida overlooking Lake Okeechobee to investigate a murder where all the evidence points to the victim's son as the killer. Holmes, however, is not so sure.

A MYSTERY IN KEY WEST

Holmes's doctor orders him to take a short holiday in Key West, and while there, Holmes is called on to look into a case in which three people involved in a Santería ritual died with no explanation.

THE CLEVER ONE

A former nun who, while still very devout, has renounced her vows so that she could "find a life, and possibly love, in the real world." She comes to Holmes in hopes that he can find out what happened to the man who promised to marry her, but mysteriously disappeared moments before their wedding.

ENIGMA IN THE REDLANDS

A nanny reaches out to Sherlock Holmes seeking his advice on whether she should take a new position when her prospective employer has demanded that she cut her hair as part of the job.

THE ADVENTURES OF SHERLOCK HOLMES IV

In this series, the original Sherlock Holmes's great-great-great grandson solves crimes and mysteries in the present day, working out of the boutique whotel he owns on South Beach.

THE RED-HAIRED MAN

A man with a shock of red hair calls on Sherlock Holmes to solve the mystery of the Red-haired League.

TOO MANY NAPOLEONS

Inspector Lestrade calls on Holmes to help him figure out why a madman would go around Miami breaking into homes and businesses to destroy cheap busts of the French Emperor. It all seems very insignificant to Holmes—until, of course, a murder occurs.

THE MISSING MAN IN THE WINDOW

In what seems to be the case of a missing person, Sherlock Holmes navigates his way through a maze of perplexing clues that leads him through a sinister world to a surprising conclusion.

THE BORNHOLM DIAMOND

A mysterious Swedish nobleman requests a meeting to discuss a matter of such serious importance that it may threaten the line of succession in one of the oldest royal houses in Europe.

THE MIDNIGHT MASS SERIES – AN AMOS FREEMAN THRILLER

MIDNIGHT MASS: THE CRIME
MIDNIGHT MASS: THE INVESTIGATION
MIDNIGHT MASS: THE BREAK
MIDNIGHT MASS: THE CHASE

It's Christmas Eve in New York. Men in hooded monks' robes and plastic masks of the face of Jesus Christ have just pulled off a spectacular robbery of the oldest church in town, getting away with tens of millions of dollars in jewelry and cash and also killing fifteen of the congregation.

Stumbling onto the scene is Lieutenant Amos Freeman, on his way home to Brooklyn after buying presents for the wife he no longer loves, and after stopping by his favorite haunt, Big Dot's Jungle Bar, for a few drinks (or as Big Dot often says, "a few too many").

Freeman snaps into professional mode, quickly assuming command of a chaotic situation, and in the process, making a big impression on a furious Mayor Frederick Lindstadt, who had been mocked and humiliated by the robbers for being not only short and bald, but helpless as well.

When the TV crews bear down and police brass arrive to take charge, Amos Freeman, not a big fan of police department politics, melts into the background, but not for long.

THE DELAPLAINE LONG WEEKEND TRAVEL GUIDE SERIES

Delaplaine Travel Guides represent the author's take on some of the many cities he's visited and many of which he has called home (for months or even years) during a lifetime of travel. The books are available as either ebooks or as printed books. Owing to the ease with which material can be uploaded, both the printed and ebook editions are updated 3 times a year.

Atlanta
Austin
Boston
Cancún (Mexico)
Cannes
Cape Cod
Charleston
Chicago
Clearwater – St. Petersburg
Fort Lauderdale
Fort Myers & Sanibel
Gettysburg
Hamptons, The
Key West & the Florida Keys
Las Vegas
Louisville
Marseille
Martha's Vineyard
Memphis
Mérida (Mexico)
Mexico City
Miami & South Beach
Milwaukee
Myrtle Beach
Nantucket
Napa Valley
Naples & Marco Island
Nashville
New Orleans
Newport (R.I.)
Philadelphia
Provincetown
Savannah
Seattle

THE FOOD ENTHUSIAST'S COMPLETE RESTAURANT GUIDES

Atlanta
Austin
Barcelona
Boston
Brooklyn
Buenos Aires
Cannes
Cape Cod
Charleston
Chicago
Florence
Fort Lauderdale
Fort Myers & Sanibel
Gettysburg
Hampton, The
Key West & the Florida Keys
Las Vegas
Lima (Peru)
London
Los Angeles
Louisville
Marseille
Martha's Vineyard
Memphis
Mérida (Mexico)
Mexico City
Miami & South Beach
Milwaukee
Napa Valley
Naples & Marco Island
Nashville
New Orleans
Newport (R.I.)
New York / Manhattan
Paris
Philadelphia
Portland (Ore.)
Provincetown
San Diego
San Juan
Savannah
Seattle
Tampa Bay

NOTES

CPSIA information can be obtained
at www.ICGtesting.com
Printed in the USA
BVHW091059130619
550826BV00012B/148/P

9 781641 873130